THE

Church

Rituals

HANDBOOK

THE Church Rituals HANDBOOK

JESSE C. MIDDENDORF

BEACON HILL PRESS
OF KANSAS CITY

Cover Design: Brandon Hill
Interior Design: Sharon Page

———

†Congregation standing
*Optional or as time allows
**Where desired, lectionary selections may be utilized according to the calendar
STTL Hymnal, *Sing to the Lord* (Kansas City: Lillenas Publishing Company, 1993)

———

Library of Congress Cataloging-in-Publication Data
The church rituals handbook / [compiled by] Jesse C. Middendorf. — 2nd ed.
   p. cm.
   Includes bibliographical references
   ISBN 978-0-8341-2457-8
   1. Church of the Nazarene—Liturgy—Texts. 2. Holiness churches—Liturgy—Texts. 3. Rites and ceremonies—Handbooks, manuals, etc. I. Middendorf, Jesse C.
BX8699.N35C48 2009
264'.0799—dc22   2009005553

10 9 8 7 6 5 4 3 2 1

To
Susan,
my wife, my friend,
my partner in ministry,
and to
Jesse A. and Martha Middendorf
who daily live the grace
embodied in ritual.

Contents

INSTALLATION SERVICES

CHURCH DEDICATIONS

OTHER RITUALS

DEVELOPMENT AND USE OF RITUAL IN PASTORAL CARE

Introduction

I welcome you to this wonderful resource for pastoral ministry. Leading the congregation in church rituals is one of the cherished privileges of being a pastor. Reflect with me for a moment, what a wondrous calling to lead a community of faith in those profound times: baptizing a new disciple of Jesus, gathering together at the Lord's Table, sharing with the couple entering the marriage covenant, sharing with the parents presenting their child for baptism or dedication, sharing with the family mourning the loss of a loved one and celebrating the hope of the resurrection, sharing as a community in worship during special seasons of the year, and more. What wondrous opportunities for the appropriation of God's amazing grace!

As you and I reflect on our own ministry, we also have the vantage point of looking across 2,000 years of Christian history. Rituals are a significant part of the story of God's people. Properly observed, rituals contribute to our being a Christian people by continuing to identify us with historic Christian faith and connect us with the church and Christians through the ages.

For the disciple of Jesus, rituals serve to remind us who we are and Whose we are. We live our lives at the intersection of two kingdoms. We live in this world as living expressions of "thy kingdom come." We are citizens of the kingdom of God engaged in the mission of God to redeem all creation, even as we are "aliens" or "exiles" in this fallen world.

As God's missionary people we live very real lives as men and women, husbands and wives, mothers and fathers, sons and daughters, friends and neighbors, employees and employers right in the midst of the raging currents of today's ever-present fallenness. And there is something gracefully powerful in our regularly engaging together in rituals that proclaim anew our real citizenship.

Part of what is happening in rituals is declaring and reenacting what it means to live in covenant with God and His people. In the imagery of Walter Brueggemann, rituals are a part of ministry that engages "exiles" in the "cadences of home." This wonderful imagery helps me to appreciate the importance of rituals. As disciples of Jesus and citizens of heaven, we live here as missional "exiles." Rituals provide precious opportunities to reenact the story of God and resonate with the "cadences of home."

Rituals contribute to the task of ministry, "to see about the alternative practices, disciplines and intentions that may sustain an alternative, subversive countercultural identity . . . the narration and nurture of a counteridentity, the enactment of the power of hope in a season of despair, and the assertion of a deep, definitional freedom from the pathologies, coercions and seductions that govern our society . . . the church [identifying and redescribing] this present place as the arena in which the rule of the creator-liberator God is working a wondrous newness."[1] We need to take every opportunity to involve our people in rituals and expose them to "cadences of home."

Sometimes we hesitate to engage in church rituals because of those around us who are not yet disciples of Jesus. We wonder if they would understand or be put off by the ritual. Yet, we believe that they, too, are "exiles" who yearn for and do not yet recognize the "cadences of home." We believe the Lord is "not wanting anyone to perish, but everyone to come to repentance" (2 Pet. 3:9, NIV). And we believe in prevenient grace—we know that the love of God is already wooing them to himself even when they are unaware.

We know that John Wesley reflected on this missional question as he considered church rituals. In one letter he poses the question this way, "What is the end of all ecclesiastical order? Is it not to bring souls from the power of Satan to God, and to build them up in His fear and love. Order, then, is so far valuable as it answers these ends; and if it answers them not, it is nothing worth."[2] Wesley appreciated the redemptive potential of ritual and encouraged the practice.

For those not yet disciples of Jesus, rituals offer a winsome opportunity to listen in on the cadences of a covenant people, to appropriate grace and to respond to God's invitation to enter into the new covenant. Brueggemann describes such "Overhearing the Good News" and suggests that it is important "to insist that such 'overhearing' is not happenstance or accidental or incidental. Rather the church, at its most courageous and its most faithful, deliberately and intentionally makes its claims for the sake of the nonchurch public."[3] Intentional rituals provide some of our greatest opportunities for "overhearing the Good News." Reflect with me again for a moment. We can tell the stories of people whose spirit resonated with the cadences as they attended a church ritual (baptism, Communion, wedding, funeral, child's dedication, pastor's installation, covenant service, etc.) and became disciples of Jesus. I wish I had space to share the story of John and Becky!

Dr. Jesse Middendorf embraces the significance of ritual

for the church, for the disciples of Jesus and those not yet disciples. He brings a wealth of experience as pastor and church leader in providing this handbook for church rituals. These rituals weave together the heart of a wonderfully gifted pastor, a keen appreciation for Christian tradition, and a sensitive awareness of the times. Keep this book close by. It will be a valuable resource as you lead people in the rituals of the church.

In addition to the rituals provided, there is also a helpful essay designed to assist in the development and use of ritual (see page 249). And for those who use the *Manual of the Church of the Nazarene,* there is also a list of the rituals included in this book that correlate with the 800 series of paragraphs in the *Manual* (see page 287).

As you participate in these rituals, may you be a blessing to God and may you appropriate the grace He so generously provides.

—Dan Copp

The Sacrament
of Baptism

THE BAPTISM OF BELIEVERS

AN EXTENDED SERVICE OF CHRISTIAN BAPTISM

THE BAPTISM OF INFANTS OR YOUNG CHILDREN

THE DEDICATION OF INFANTS OR YOUNG CHILDREN

THE DEDICATION OF INFANTS OR YOUNG CHILDREN
(Ritual for Single Parent or Guardian)

THE BLESSING OF ADOPTION AND DEDICATION

THE BAPTISM OF BELIEVERS

DEARLY BELOVED: Baptism is the sign and seal of the new covenant of grace, the significance of which is attested by the apostle Paul in his letter to the Romans as follows:

"Or don't you know that all of us who were baptized into Christ Jesus were baptized into his death? We were therefore buried with him through baptism into death in order that, just as Christ was raised from the dead through the glory of the Father, we too may live a new life. If we have been united with him like this in his death, we will certainly also be united with him in his resurrection" (Rom. 6:3-5, NIV).

The earliest and simplest statement of Christian belief, into which you now come to be baptized, is the Apostles' Creed, which reads as follows:

"I believe in God the Father Almighty, Maker of heaven and earth;

"And in Jesus Christ, His only Son, our Lord; who was conceived by the Holy Ghost, born of the Virgin Mary, suffered under Pontius Pilate, was crucified, dead, and buried; He descended into hell; the third day He rose again from the dead; He ascended into heaven, and sitteth at the right hand of God the Father Almighty; from thence He shall come to judge the quick and the dead.

"I believe in the Holy Ghost, the holy Church of Jesus Christ, the communion of saints, the forgiveness of sins, the resurrection of the body, and the life everlasting."

Will you be baptized into this faith? If so, answer, "I will."

Response: I will.

Do you acknowledge Jesus Christ as your personal Savior, and do you realize that He saves you now?

Response: I do.

Will you obey God's holy will and keep His commandments, walking in them all the days of your life?

Response: I will.

The minister, giving the full name of the person and using the preferred form of baptism—sprinkling, pouring, or immersion—shall say:

_____ , I baptize thee in the name of the Father, and of the Son, and of the Holy Spirit. Amen.

AN EXTENDED SERVICE OF CHRISTIAN BAPTISM

The following service order may be followed where a more expansive service is desired.

GATHERING
Prelude

INTRODUCTION TO THE SERVICE

As candidates for baptism come forward, an appropriate hymn of worship or testimony may be sung.

When the candidates are in place, the minister may make the following statement to the congregation:

DEAR FRIENDS: Through the sacrament of baptism, our entrance into the Body of Christ through the new birth is given visible expression. Having been incorporated into God's mighty act of salvation in Christ, we follow Him in baptism, publicly identifying with Him and testifying to our having appropriated by faith the benefits of the atonement that Christ has provided us in His suffering, death, and resurrection.

We join these persons in a celebration of the grace of God in their lives and unite our hearts in praise to the Father, the Son, and the Holy Spirit.

PRESENTATION OF THE CANDIDATES

A representative of the congregation presents the candidates to the minister and the congregation with appropriate statements:

I present _____ for baptism.

PROCLAMATION OF THE WORD OR TESTIMONY OF CANDIDATES

At this point in the service, a sermon regarding the significance of baptism may be preached, or the candidates may give a personal testimony to their Christian faith and experience. Where a small class of candidates is presented or time permits, both may be included.

RENUNCIATION OF SIN AND PROFESSION OF FAITH

The vows of Christian baptism have consisted, from the earliest periods of the Church, in a personal renunciation of sin and profession of faith. The minister may here address the candidates and ask them for their avowals of faith and obedience as follows:

On behalf of Christ and the Church, I ask you:

Do you renounce Satan and all the spiritual forces of wickedness that rebel against God?

Response: I renounce them.

Do you renounce the evil powers of this world that corrupt and that destroy the creatures of God?

Response: I renounce them.

Do you renounce sinful desires that draw you from the love of God?

Response: I renounce them.

Have you repented of your sins, turned to Christ, and accepted Him as your Savior?

Response: I have.

Have you put your whole trust in His grace alone for your redemption?

Response: I have.

Do you promise to follow and obey Him as your redeeming Lord?

Response: I do.

After the candidates have responded, the minister addresses the congregation, saying:

Will you who witness these vows do all in your power to support *these persons* in *their* life in Christ? Will you pray for them, encourage them, instruct and lead them, and will you so live before them that they may follow your example in Christian living?

People: We will.

The minister then says these or similar words to the congregation and the candidates:

Let us join *those* who *are* following Christ in baptism and reaffirm our faith.

Minister: Do you believe in God the Father?

21

People: I believe in God, the Father Almighty, Creator of heaven and earth.

Minister: Do you believe in Jesus Christ, the Son of God?

People: I believe in Jesus Christ, His only Son, our Lord, who was conceived by the Holy Spirit, born of the Virgin Mary, suffered under Pontius Pilate, was crucified, dead, and buried; He descended to the dead; the third day He rose again from the dead; He ascended into heaven, and sitteth at the right hand of God the Father Almighty; from thence He shall come to judge the living and the dead.

Minister: Do you believe in God the Holy Spirit?

People: I believe in the Holy Spirit, the holy Church universal, the communion of saints, the forgiveness of sins, the resurrection of the body, and the life everlasting.

Minister: Will you continue in the apostles' teaching and fellowship, in the breaking of bread, and in prayer?

People: I will, with God's help.

Minister: Will you continue in resisting evil, and, should you fall into sin, will you repent and turn to the Lord?

People: I will, with God's help.

Minister: Will you proclaim by word and example the good news of God in Christ?

People: I will, with God's help.

Minister: Will you earnestly seek to purify yourself from everything that contaminates body and spirit, perfecting holiness out of reverence for Christ?

People: I will, with God's help.

Minister: Will you serve the present age, fulfilling in your life and ministry the call of Christ to make disciples of all nations?

People: I will, with God's help.

BAPTISM OF CANDIDATES

Candidates are ushered to the water by sponsors or congregational assistants. The chosen mode of baptism is administered, the minister using the given name of the candidate as follows:

_____ , I baptize you in the name of the Father and of the Son and of the Holy Spirit. Amen.

WELCOME OF THE NEWLY BAPTIZED BY THE CONGREGATION

Pastor: Let us welcome the newly baptized.

People: We receive you into the household of God. Confess the faith of Christ crucified, proclaim His resurrection, and share with us in His eternal priesthood.

DOXOLOGY

BENEDICTION

THE BAPTISM OF INFANTS
OR YOUNG CHILDREN

The original ritual for "The Baptism of Infants" appeared in the *Manual of the Church of the Nazarene* from 1908 to 1968. It was utilized as the only ritual regarding infants or young children until 1936. At that time a ritual for "The Dedication of Infants or Young Children" was added, along with the original rite for "The Baptism of Infants." In 1972 the ritual for "The Baptism of Infants" was removed from the *Manual,* and language for baptism was edited into the ritual for "The Dedication of Infants or Young Children." In 1980 a new ritual for "The Baptism of Young Children" was included in the ritual portion of the *Manual,* and the combination language was removed from the ritual for "The Dedication of Infants or Young Children."

While there are those within the Wesleyan-Holiness tradition who disagree with the practice of infant baptism in favor of "believers' baptism," those who support infant baptism do so in the belief that there is scriptural, theological, and historical warrant for the practice.

There are New Testament scriptures that make reference to the baptism of "households," implying the inclusion of all the members of the family, according to the interpretations of many scholars (Acts 16:15, 33; 1 Cor. 1:16). "Household baptisms, strengthened by such adjectives as *holos* (whole) and *pas* (all) and *hapartes* (entire, a strengthened form of *pas*), strongly imply that infants were baptized in these instances. Families were solidarities then, and the decisions of the father

24

settled important matters for all others members of the family. This had long obtained in Judaism, and it obtained in the Gentile community of the first century."[4]

The Church of the Nazarene gives clear expression to its belief that young children are covered under the Atonement. The article of faith in the *Manual* on the Atonement (6) states: "The Atonement is graciously efficacious for the salvation of the irresponsible and for the children in innocency but is efficacious for the salvation of those who reach the age of responsibility only when they repent and believe."[5] It is certain that God's prevenient grace is already at work in the life of a young child, which gives warrant to the practice of infant baptism as a declaration of this prevenient grace.

And infant baptism further declares the covenant relationship that exists between Christ and the Church on the basis of the Atonement. Children who are baptized are included in the covenant community, declared in public rite to have been included in the finished work of Christ on the Cross. As one theologian has put it, "As a sacrament, baptism is not a purely personal matter between an individual and God. It is a sacrament of the Church. This means that the baptized person belongs to a fellowship. Christ came to overcome human isolation (1 John 1:3), and Christian life can be meaningful only in the fellowship of others. In baptizing infants, the Church is saying that the child is included in the fellowship, is a part of the Body, is under the covenant."[6]

H. Ray Dunning goes on to say, "Furthermore, a genuine validity can be attached to infant baptism if it is seen as the induction of the child into the covenant community with a concomitant commitment of the community to help guide the child 'in the nurture and admonition of the Lord' (Eph. 6:4,

KJV). It might, in fact, militate against the loss of children from the church by guarding against the church becoming spectators until the child experiences an adult conversion."[7]

Theologians within the Wesleyan-Holiness tradition have given wide acknowledgment to the theological validity of infant baptism. Familiar names such as Wakefield, Wiley, Grider, Dunning, and Staples have expressed the significance of the practice and given theological rationale from a wide array of perspectives. Each has also appealed to the historical precedence, many citing evidences of the practice among the apostles and certainty of its inclusion in church practice before the end of the third century.

Perhaps the most eloquent expression of the intent of infant baptism is in the words of Dr. Rob Staples:

> From the moment of baptism, as the baptized child grows and develops toward maturity, the parents and the Church are under solemn obligation to use every means available to communicate to the young person this Good News: "When you were too young to walk, we carried you in our arms. Likewise when you were too young to choose to be a part of the Body of Christ, we chose for you. We brought you into the fellowship, and you were incorporated into the Body. Now you will need to decide whether you will choose for yourself that which was chosen for you. We pray that you will choose it and not reject it."[8]

Knowing that it is not our faith but God's grace that saves us, in baptism, both for infants and believers, we celebrate God's prior grace toward us. Only secondarily and consequentially do we show through baptism our active response to God.

Having that confidence, the Wesleyan-Holiness tradition has embraced the practice of infant baptism, and the following rituals are included for the use of those parents who desire this sacred rite.

Included in this format is a suggested introduction to the rite of infant baptism that might be read in those churches who are less familiar with the practice. It expresses both the confidence that the ritual has significance to the church as well as the child and the expressed desire for the church to accept its responsibility to assist the child in his or her growth toward spiritual maturity and a personal affirmation of faith in Christ as the source of our redemption.

Following are both the original ritual for "The Baptism of Infants" and the later ritual for "The Baptism of Young Children." Following the rituals for baptism of children will be found the current *Manual* rituals for "The Dedication of Infants or Young Children."

The following introduction may be utilized where a congregation is unfamiliar with the ritual of infant baptism, giving a brief background for the practice and a rationale for its place in the life of an evangelical congregation.

The Church has always understood the necessity for parents to make important choices for the spiritual welfare and development of their children. Among those is the choice of whether to offer their children to God in infant dedication or to request the pastor to administer the sacrament of infant baptism to their children. Many churches hold that either is an appropriate choice, but that the parents should make the decision with the counsel and guidance of family and pastor.

For those who choose infant baptism, many churches hold that there is a significant moment of grace involved, not that we convey grace in the sacrament, but that we proclaim the prevenient grace of God that covers this child from the time of birth, and even before. It is a symbol of the covenant that exists between God and the Church. In this rite we are indicating that we believe that God has incorporated this child into His Body by prevenient grace. But we are not determining for this child what his (her) choices will be later in life.

There will come a time when these parents must say to this child, "When you were too young to walk, we carried you in our arms. Likewise, when you were too young to choose to be a part of the Body of Christ, we chose for you. We brought you into the fellowship, and you were incorporated into the Body. Now you will need to decide whether you will choose for yourself that which was chosen for you. We pray that you will choose it, and not reject it."[9]

When an infant or young child has been baptized, it is right and necessary that when he or she comes to maturity, he or she be led to make his or her own very personal confession in Christ.

But today we celebrate that God in His prevenient grace has embraced this child in the covenant He has

28

made with His people. We, as the people of God, have an obligation to nurture his (her) growth toward maturity and a personal love for Christ. This is God's child, and we are responsible for telling him (her) that as he (she) grows to maturity and accountability. Then, when he (she) is able to make the choice for himself (herself), he (she) may choose to embrace Christ by personal faith and continue in that grace.

Join me now as we participate in this sacred rite of baptism of a child.

Rite One

The family is invited to join the ministers at the front of the sanctuary, the child in the arms of a parent or guardian. The minister, facing the family and the congregation, shall read the following:

DEARLY BELOVED: Baptism is the external seal of the new covenant of grace. In presenting this child for Christian baptism, you must remember that it is your part and duty to see that he (she) be taught, as soon as he (she) shall be able to learn, the nature and the end of this holy sacrament. You shall call upon him (her) to give reverent attendance upon appointed means of grace; see that he (she) is taught the truth of God as contained in the Holy Scriptures, and help him (her) as you may be able in the way of life.

The minister may then ask the parents or guardians of the child to name the child and baptize him (her), saying:

_____ , I baptize thee in the name of the Father and of the Son and of the Holy Ghost. Amen.

The minister may offer prayer, the congregation uniting in the Lord's Prayer.

Rite Two

When the sponsors shall have presented themselves with the child (or children) the minister shall say:

DEARLY BELOVED: While we do not hold that baptism imparts the regenerating grace of God, we do believe that Christ gave this holy sacrament as a sign and seal of the new covenant. Christian baptism signifies for this young child God's gracious acceptance on the basis of His prevenient grace in Christ, and points forward to his (her) personal appropriation of the benefits of the Atonement when he (she) reaches the age of moral accountability and exercises conscious saving faith in Jesus Christ.

In presenting this child for baptism you are hereby witnessing to your own personal Christian faith and to your purpose to guide him (her) early in life to a knowledge of Christ as Savior. To this end it is your duty to teach him (her), as soon as he (she) shall be able to learn, the nature and end of this holy sacrament; to watch over his (her) education, that he (she) may not be led astray; to direct his (her) feet to the sanctuary; to restrain him (her) from evil associates and habits; and as much as in you lies, to bring him (her) up in the nurture and admonition of the Lord.

Will you endeavor to do so by the help of God? If so, answer, "I will."

The minister may then ask the parents or guardians to name the child and shall then baptize the child, repeating his (her) full name and saying:

_____ , I baptize thee in the name of the Father, and of the Son, and of the Holy Spirit. Amen.

The minister may then offer the following prayer or may use an extemporary prayer:

Heavenly Father, we humbly pray that Thou wilt take this child into Thy loving care. Abundantly enrich him (her) with Thy heavenly grace; bring him (her) safely through the perils of childhood; deliver him (her) from the temptations of youth; lead him (her) to a personal knowledge of Christ as Savior; help him (her) to grow in wisdom, and in stature, and in favor with God and man, and to persevere therein to the end. Uphold the parents with loving care, that with wise counsel and holy example they may faithfully discharge their responsibilities to both this child and to Thee. In the name of Jesus Christ our Lord. Amen.

THE DEDICATION OF INFANTS OR YOUNG CHILDREN

When the parents or guardians have presented themselves with the child (or children) the minister shall say:

"Then little children were brought to Jesus for him to place his hands on them and pray for them. But the disciples rebuked those who brought them. Jesus said, 'Let the little children come to me, and do not hinder them, for the kingdom of heaven belongs to such as these'" (Matt. 19:13-14, NIV).

In presenting this child for dedication you signify not only your faith in the Christian religion but also your desire that he (she) may early know and follow the will of God, may live and die a Christian, and come unto everlasting blessedness.

In order to attain this holy end, it will be your duty, as parents (guardians), to teach him (her) early the fear of the Lord, to watch over his (her) education, that he (she) be not led astray; to direct his (her) youthful mind to the Holy Scriptures and his (her) feet to the sanctuary; to restrain him (her) from evil associates and habits; and, as much as in you lies, to bring him (her) up in the nurture and admonition of the Lord.

Will you endeavor to do so by the help of God? If so, answer, "I will."

Response: I will.

Pastor: I now ask you, the congregation; will you commit yourself as the Body of Christ to support and encourage these parents as they endeavor to fulfill their responsibilities to this child and to assist _____ by nurturing his (her) growth toward spiritual maturity?

Response: We will.

Pastor: Our loving Heavenly Father, we do here and now dedicate _____ in the name of the Father, and of the Son, and of the Holy Spirit. Amen.

Then the minister may offer the following prayer or may use an extemporary prayer:

Heavenly Father, we humbly pray that Thou wilt take this child into Thy loving care. Abundantly enrich him (her) with Thy heavenly grace; bring him (her) safely through the perils of childhood; deliver him (her) from the temptations of youth; lead him (her) to a personal knowledge of Christ as Savior; help him (her) to grow in wisdom, and in stature, and in favor with God and man, and to persevere therein to the end. Uphold the parents with loving care, that with wise counsel and holy example they may faithfully discharge their responsibilities both to this child and to Thee. In the name of Jesus Christ our Lord. Amen.

THE DEDICATION OF INFANTS OR YOUNG CHILDREN

Ritual for Single Parent or Guardian

When the parent or guardian has presented himself (herself) with the child (or children) the minister shall say:

"Then little children were brought to Jesus for him to place his hands on them and pray for them. But the disciples rebuked those who brought them. Jesus said, 'Let the little children come to me, and do not hinder them, for the kingdom of heaven belongs to such as these'" (Matt. 19:13-14, NIV).

In presenting this child for dedication you signify not only your faith in the Christian religion but also your desire that he (she) may early know and follow the will of God, may live and die a Christian, and come unto everlasting blessedness.

In order to attain this holy end, it will be your duty, as a parent (guardian), to teach him (her) early the fear of the Lord, to watch over his (her) education, that he (she) be not led astray; to direct his (her) youthful mind to the Holy Scriptures, and his (her) feet to the sanctuary; to restrain him (her) from evil associates and habits; and, as much as in you lies, to bring him/her up in the nurture and admonition of the Lord.

Will you endeavor to do so by the help of God? If so, answer, "I will."

Response: I will.

Pastor: I now ask you, the congregation; will you commit yourself as the Body of Christ to support and encourage this parent as he (she) endeavors to fulfill his (her) responsibilities to this child and to assist _____ by nurturing his (her) growth toward spiritual maturity?

Response: We will.

Pastor: Our loving Heavenly Father, we do here and now dedicate _____ in the name of the Father, and of the Son, and of the Holy Spirit. Amen.

Then the minister may offer the following prayer or may use an extemporary prayer:

Heavenly Father, we humbly pray that Thou wilt take this child into Thy loving care. Abundantly enrich him (her) with Thy heavenly grace; bring him (her) safely through the perils of childhood; deliver him (her) from the temptations of youth; lead him (her) to a personal knowledge of Christ as Savior; help him (her) to grow in wisdom, and in stature, and in favor with God and man, and to persevere therein to the end. Uphold the parent with loving care, that with wise counsel and holy example he (she) may faithfully discharge his (her) responsibilities both to this child and to Thee. In the name of Jesus Christ our Lord. Amen.

THE BLESSING OF ADOPTION AND DEDICATION

This ritual is designed to provide an adopting family a means to participate in a public expression of their desires for the spiritual welfare of their child. The ritual does this through the dedication of the child, as well as the public declaration of the family's covenant relationship with the adopted child.

The family is invited by the pastor to present themselves before the congregation with their child. Extended family members may be invited to participate, providing them all a means to express publically their covenant bond with the adopted child (or children).

The pastor (or other participant) may read the following passage of Scripture: "I prayed for this child, and the LORD has granted me what I asked of him. So now, I give him [her] to the LORD. For his [her] whole life he [she] will be given over to the LORD" (1 Sam. 1:27-28, NIV).

Pastor: Your child is a gift of God to you, as fully your own as if born from your own body. Your presentation of this child to God in dedication is also an expression of your covenant relationship with this child. It is based on the pattern of the love of God for us all, a love without limit, without condition, and without ending.

In presenting your child before the Lord today, you are making a public expression of your faith in the Christian religion and your desire that _____ *[name of child]* may early in life come to know and follow the will of God, may live and die a Christian, and come unto everlasting blessing.

In order to attain this holy end, it will be your duty as parents to teach him (her) early in life to reverently fear the Lord, to watch over his (her) education that he (she) not be led astray, to direct his (her) mind to the Holy Scriptures, and his (her) feet to the sanctuary, to restrain him (her) from evil associates and habits, and as much as in you lies, to bring him (her) up in the nurture and admonition of the Lord.

Parents, will you endeavor to do these things, by the grace and help of God? If so, please answer, "We will."

Response: We will.

Pastor: I now ask you, the congregation: will you commit yourself as the Body of Christ, adopted into His family by grace through faith, to support and encourage these parents as they endeavor to fulfill their responsibility as parents to this child? Will you lovingly and fully accept this child as a gift of God to this family and this congregation, and will you assist _____ *[name of child]* by nurturing his (her) growth toward spiritual maturity?

If you will do so, please respond, "We will."

Response: We will.

Pastor: Our loving Heavenly Father, we do here and

now dedicate to You _____ in the name of the Father, and of the Son, and of the Holy Spirit. Amen.

Then the minister may offer the following prayer or may use an extemporary prayer:

Heavenly Father, we present to You today this gift from Your hands to this family. We ask You to enrich _____ with Your grace and mercy. Bring him (her) safely through the experiences of childhood, deliver him (her) from the temptations of youth; lead him (her) to a personal knowledge of Christ as Savior; help him (her) to grow in wisdom, and in stature, and in favor with God and man, and to persevere to the end. Uphold these parents with Your loving care and wisdom. Grant them the patience and grace to be the example of holiness they desire to be. May their covenant of love, to which they give witness today, endure all of the tests and stresses of life as they embrace this gift from Your hands. May they faithfully discharge their duties as parents to their child and keep their promise of covenant love with You.

The Reception of Church Members

THE RECEPTION OF
CHURCH MEMBERS

The prospective members having come forward to stand before the altar of the church, the pastor shall address them as follows:

DEARLY BELOVED: The privileges and blessings that we have in association together in the Church of Jesus Christ are very sacred and precious. There is in it such hallowed fellowship as cannot otherwise be known.

There is such helpfulness with brotherly watch care and counsel as can be found only in the Church.

There is the godly care of pastors, with the teachings of the Word; and the helpful inspiration of social worship. And there is cooperation in service, accomplishing that which cannot otherwise be done.

The doctrines upon which the church rests as essential to Christian experience are brief.

We believe in God the Father, Son, and Holy Spirit. We especially emphasize the deity of Jesus Christ and the personality of the Holy Spirit.

We believe that human beings are born in sin; that they need the work of forgiveness through Christ and the new birth by the Holy Spirit; that subsequent to this there is the deeper work of heart cleansing or entire sanctification through the infilling of the Holy Spirit, and that to each of these works of grace the Holy Spirit gives witness.

We believe that our Lord will return, the dead shall be raised, and that all shall come to final judgment with its rewards and punishments.

Do you heartily believe these truths? If so, answer, "I do."

Response: I do.

Pastor: Do you acknowledge Jesus Christ as your personal Savior, and do you realize that He saves you now?

Response: I do.

Pastor: Desiring to unite with the Church of the Nazarene, do you covenant to give yourself to the fellowship and work of God in connection with it, as set forth in the General Rules and Special Rules of the Church of the Nazarene? Will you endeavor in every way to glorify God, by a humble walk, godly conversation, and holy service; by devotedly giving of your means; by faithful attendance upon the means of grace; and, abstaining from all evil, will you seek earnestly to perfect holiness of heart and life in the fear of the Lord?

Response: I will.

Pastor: I welcome you into this church, to its sacred fellowship, responsibilities, and privileges. May the great Head of the Church bless and keep you and enable you to be faithful in all good works, that your life and witness may be effective in leading others to Christ.

The minister shall then take each one by the hand, and with appropriate words of personal greeting welcome each into the church.

Alternate form for members joining by letter of transfer:

_____ , formerly a member (members) of the Church of the Nazarene at _____ , comes (come) to join the fellowship of this local congregation.

Taking each by the hand, or speaking to the group, the minister shall say:

It gives me pleasure on behalf of this church to welcome you into our membership. We trust that we will be a source of encouragement and strength to you and that you, in turn, will be a source of blessing and help to us. May the Lord richly bless you in the salvation of souls and in the advancement of His kingdom.

The Sacrament of the Lord's Supper

THE SACRAMENT OF THE LORD'S SUPPER

COMMUNION UNDER SPECIAL CIRCUMSTANCES

THE SACRAMENT OF
THE LORD'S SUPPER

Rite One

The administration of the Lord's Supper may be introduced by an appropriate sermon and the reading of 1 Cor. 11:23-29; Luke 22:14-20, or some other suitable passage. Let the minister then give the following invitation:

The Lord himself ordained this holy sacrament. He commanded His disciples to partake of the bread and wine, emblems of His broken body and shed blood. This is His table. The feast is for His disciples. Let all those who have with true repentance forsaken their sins, and have believed in Christ unto salvation, draw near and take these emblems, and, by faith, partake of the life of Jesus Christ, to your soul's comfort and joy. Let us remember that it is the memorial of the death and passion of our Lord; also a token of His coming again. Let us not forget that we are one, at one table with the Lord.

The minister may offer a prayer of confession and supplication, concluding with the following prayer of consecration:

Almighty God, our Heavenly Father, who of Thy tender mercy didst give Thine only Son, Jesus Christ, to suffer death upon the Cross for our redemption: hear us, we most humbly beseech Thee. Grant that, as we receive these Thy creatures of bread and wine according to the holy institution of Thy Son, our Savior Jesus Christ, in remembrance of His passion and death, we may be made partakers of the benefits of His atoning sacrifice.

We are reminded that in the same night that our Lord was betrayed, He took bread and, when He had given thanks, He broke it and gave it to His disciples, saying, "This is my body given for you; do this in remembrance of me" (1 Cor. 11:24, NIV). Likewise, after supper, He took the cup, and when He had given thanks, He gave it to them, saying, "This cup is the new covenant in my blood, which is poured out for you (Luke 22:20, NIV); do this, whenever you drink it, in remembrance of me" (1 Cor. 11:25, NIV).

May we come before Thee in true humility and faith as we partake of this holy sacrament. Through Jesus Christ our Lord. Amen.

> Then may the minister, partaking first, with the assistance of any other ministers present, and when necessary, of the stewards, administer the Communion to the people.

> While the bread is being distributed, let the minister say:

The body of our Lord Jesus Christ, which was broken for you, preserve you blameless, unto everlasting life. Take and eat this, in remembrance that Christ died for you.

As the cup is being passed, let the minister say:

The blood of our Lord Jesus Christ, which was shed for you, preserve you blameless unto everlasting life. Drink this, in remembrance that Christ's blood was shed for you, and be thankful.

After all have partaken, the minister may then offer a concluding prayer of thanksgiving and commitment (34.5, 413.4, 413.11, 427.7, 428.2, 429.1, *Manual,* Church of the Nazarene, 2005-9).

Rite Two

The following more detailed order of service may be utilized when desired:

A Service of Word and Table

SERVICE OF THE WORD

PRELUDE

Leader: O worship the LORD in the beauty of holiness;

People: Let the whole earth stand in awe of Him.

All: "Almighty God, unto whom all hearts are open,

all desires known, and from whom no secrets are hidden: Cleanse the thoughts of our hearts by the inspiration of Your Holy Spirit, that we may perfectly love You and worthily magnify Your holy name; through Jesus Christ our Lord. Amen."[10]

PROCESSIONAL*

†HYMN

OLD TESTAMENT LESSON:

> Appropriate lesson selected to coincide with the significance of the service or the meaning of the Passover as it is related to the sacrifice of Christ**

HYMN*

PSALM:

> A selected psalm, portion of a psalm, or other Old Testament wisdom literature, perhaps arranged as a responsive reading for congregational participation**

EPISTLE LESSON:

> Appropriate lesson selected to coincide with the significance of the service or the meaning of the Lord's Supper**

HYMN*

†GOSPEL LESSON:

> Appropriate lesson selected to coincide with the significance of the service or the meaning of the Lord's Supper**

SERMON:

THE NICENE CREED:

If desired, the Apostles' Creed may be used.

All: "We believe in one God, the Father, the Almighty, Maker of heaven and earth, of all that is, seen and unseen.

We believe in one Lord, Jesus Christ, the only Son of God, eternally begotten of the Father, God from God, Light from Light, true God from true God, begotten, not made, of one Being with the Father. Through him all things were made. For us and for our salvation he came down from heaven: by the power of the Holy Spirit he became incarnate from the Virgin Mary, and was made man. For our sake he was crucified under Pontius Pilate; he suffered death and was buried. On the third day he rose again in accordance with the Scriptures; he ascended into heaven and is seated at the right hand of the Father. He will come again in glory to judge the living and the dead, and his kingdom will have no end.

We believe in the Holy Spirit, the Lord, the Giver of life, who proceeds from the Father and the Son. With the Father and the Son he is worshiped and glorified. He has spoken through the Prophets.

We believe in one holy catholic and apostolic Church. We acknowledge one baptism for the forgiveness of sins. We look for the resurrection of the dead and the life of the world to come. Amen."

PRAYERS OF THE PEOPLE

COMMUNITY LIFE AND ANNOUNCEMENTS

GIVING OF TITHES AND FREEWILL OFFERINGS

†THE DOXOLOGY

> If desired, during the singing of the Doxology, the elements of the Lord's Supper may be brought to the table of the Lord in preparation for distribution. Once the elements are placed on the table, the congregation standing, the minister may lead the following:

Minister: The Lord be with you.

People: And also with you.

Minister: Lift up your hearts.

People: We lift them up to the Lord.

Minister: Let us give thanks to the Lord our God.

People: It is right to give God thanks and praise.

Minister: It is right and a good and joyful thing, always and everywhere to give thanks to You, Father Almighty, Creator of heaven and earth. Grant to us, Lord, we pray, the spirit to think and do always the things that are right, that we, because we cannot exist without You, may be enabled to live according to Your will; through Jesus Christ, our Lord, who lives and reigns with You and the Holy Spirit, one God, now and forever. Amen.

All: Holy, holy, holy, Lord God of power and might,

heaven and earth are full of Your glory. Hosanna in the highest. Blessed is he who comes in the name of the Lord. Hosanna in the highest.

Congregation may be seated

PRAYER OF CONSECRATION:

The minister may pray extempore, or the following may be used:

Minister: We acclaim You, holy Lord, glorious in power. Your mighty works reveal Your wisdom and love. You formed us in Your own image, giving the whole world into our care, so that we might serve all Your creation. When our disobedience took us far from You, You did not abandon us to the power of death. In Your mercy You came to our help, so that in seeking You we might find You. Through the prophets You taught us to hope for salvation. You sent Your only Son to be our Savior. And, that we might no longer live for ourselves, but for Him who died and was raised for us, You sent the Holy Spirit, Christ's first gift for those who believe, to complete His work in the world and to bring to fulfillment the sanctification of us all.

The minister, placing a hand on the bread, may pray:

When the hour had come for Him to be glorified by You, Heavenly Father, our Lord Jesus Christ took bread; and when He had given thanks to You, He broke it, and gave it to His disciples, and said, "Take, eat: this is my body, which is broken for you: this do in remembrance of me" (1 Cor. 11:24).

Placing a hand on the cup, the minister may pray:

After supper He took the cup of wine; and when He had given thanks, He gave it to them and said, "Drink from it, all of you. This is my blood of the covenant, which is poured out for many for the forgiveness of sins" (Matt. 26:27-28, NIV). "Do this, whenever you drink it, in remembrance of me" (1 Cor. 11:25, NIV).

Minister: Therefore, according to His command, O Father,

People: We remember His death, we proclaim His resurrection, we rejoice in His gift of the Holy Spirit.

Minister: Lord, we pray that in Your goodness and mercy, Your Holy Spirit may descend upon us, and upon these gifts, sanctifying them and showing them to be holy gifts for Your holy people, the bread of life and the cup of salvation, the body and blood of Your Son, Jesus Christ.

Grant that all who share this bread and cup may become one body and one spirit, a living sacrifice in Christ, to the praise of Your name.

All this we ask through Your Son, Jesus Christ. By Him and with Him and in Him, in the unity of the Holy Spirit all honor and glory is Yours, Almighty Father, now and forever. Amen.

And now, as our Savior Christ has taught us, we pray:

All: Our Father, who art in heaven, hallowed be thy name. Thy kingdom come, thy will be done, on earth as it is in heaven. Give us this day our daily bread. And forgive us our trespasses, as we forgive those who trespass against us. And lead us not into temptation, but deliver us from evil. For thine is the kingdom and the power and the glory for ever. Amen (see Matt. 6:9-13).

If desired, the minister may hold a piece of the unleavened bread and cup of the juice of the vine and say:

Minister: Christ our Passover is sacrificed for us.

People: Therefore, let us keep the feast. Alleluia!

Minister: The gifts of God for the people of God. Take them in remembrance that Christ died for you, and feed on Him in your hearts by faith with thanksgiving.

All who confess Jesus Christ as Lord are welcome to come to His table.

Methods of serving the elements of the Lord's Supper vary. The congregation may be invited to the altar of the church, to be served by the elders of the church, assisted by others as prescribed in church polity.

The elements may be served by distributing trays containing the bread and wine to the seated congregation.

The elements may be served by the method of intinction. In this method, the minister stands at the altar or the table, holding a tray with pieces of unleavened Communion bread in one hand and a chalice or cup of juice of the grape in the other. The congregation files before the minister, each participant taking a piece of the bread and dipping it into the cup, and then eating the bread. The participant may then either kneel for a time at the altar or return to the pew for meditation and prayer while others are being served.

After all who desire to participate have been served, the minister shall continue.

Minister: Let us pray.

All: Almighty and ever living God, we thank You for feeding us with the spiritual food of the body and blood of Your Son, our Savior Jesus Christ; and for assuring us that we are living members of His body. And now, Father, send us out to do the work You have given us to do, to love and serve You as faithful witnesses of Christ our Lord. To Him, to You, and to the Holy Spirit, be honor and glory, now and forever. Amen.

†Hymn

Recessional*

Benediction: Now "may the God of peace . . . sanctify you entirely; and may your spirit and soul and body be kept sound and blameless at the coming of our Lord Jesus Christ. The one who calls you is faithful, and he will do this" (1 Thess. 5:23-24, nrsv). Amen.

Postlude

COMMUNION UNDER
SPECIAL CIRCUMSTANCES

This form is intended for use when there are those who are not able, because of health or other extenuating circumstances, to participate in the Communion of the Lord's Supper with the congregation.

When persons are unable to participate with the congregation for extended periods of time, it is desirable that the pastor or other appropriate minister designee arrange to celebrate the Lord's Supper with them on a regular basis, wherever it is best suited to meet needs of the participants.

This form, or the form found in Rite One, would be appropriate for use.

When possible, members of the family, relatives, or friends from the congregation may be invited to join in the celebration of the Lord's Supper.

The celebration may begin with the following:

Almighty God, unto whom all hearts are open, all desires known, and from whom no secrets are hidden: Cleanse the thoughts of our hearts by the inspiration of Your Holy Spirit, that we may perfectly love You and worthily magnify Your holy name; through Jesus Christ our Lord. Amen.[11]

The minister may read a passage of Scripture from the

Gospel and other scriptures deemed appropriate for the occasion. One of the following may be read:

John 3:16

John 6:35

John 6:51, 55-56

John 15:4-5, 8-9

After reading the scriptures, the minister may comment on them briefly.

The minister may then pray a prayer of confession and supplication. The following may be used:

Father of Grace and Mercy, we come humbly before You in preparation for our participation in the holy sacrament of the Lord's Supper. We come in grateful recognition of Your love for us, as demonstrated in the gift of Your Son, Jesus Christ, for our redemption.

We humbly remember how we lived apart from Your grace, resisting Your love, and deserving nothing of Your mercies. And yet You extended Your gracious provision for our redemption through the suffering of Your Son, Jesus Christ, our Lord.

Grant to us a renewed appreciation for Your mercies. May the sufferings of Jesus on our behalf be embraced with faith and thanksgiving by all who are here. And may Your Holy Spirit accomplish in us that which is pleasing and acceptable to You, through Jesus Christ our Lord who, with You and the Holy Spirit, reigns in heaven and on earth, one God, Father, Son, and Holy Spirit. Amen.

If desired, the minister may invite those present to pray the Lord's Prayer, as follows:

Let us pray in the words our Savior Christ has taught us:

"Our Father, who art in heaven, hallowed be thy name. Thy kingdom come, thy will be done, on earth as it is in heaven.

"Give us this day our daily bread. And forgive us our trespasses, as we forgive those who trespass against us.

"And lead us not into temptation, but deliver us from evil.

"For thine is the kingdom and the power and the glory for ever. Amen" (see Matt. 6:9-13).

The minister may then pray a prayer of consecration of the elements of the sacrament. The following may be used if desired:

Heavenly Father, by Your mercy You gave Your only Son, Jesus Christ, to endure the sufferings on Calvary for our redemption. Hear us, we pray, that these emblems of bread and wine may become for us the representations of His body and blood, that we may be partakers of the benefits of His atoning sacrifice on our behalf.

We remember that in the same night that He was betrayed, our Lord took bread and, when He had given thanks, broke it and gave it to His disciples, saying, "Take, eat: this is my body, which is broken for you: this do in remembrance of me" (1 Cor. 11:24). In like manner, after supper, He took the cup, and when He had given thanks, He gave it to them, saying, "Drink from it, all of you. This is my blood of the covenant, which is poured out for many for the forgiveness of sins" (Matt. 26:27-28, NIV). "Do this, whenever you drink it, in remembrance of me" (1 Cor. 11:25, NIV).

May we come before You in true humility and faith as we partake of this holy sacrament. Through Jesus Christ our Lord. Amen.

The minister may say the following invitation:

The gifts of God for the people of God.

And may add:

Take them in remembrance that Christ died for you, and feed on Him in your hearts by faith with thanksgiving.

The sacrament is administered with the following or other words:

The body (blood) of our Lord Jesus Christ, given for you. His grace keep you in everlasting life. [Amen.]

Or:

The body (blood) of our Lord Jesus Christ, which

was given for you, preserve you blameless unto everlasting life. Take this in remembrance that Christ suffered for you, and be thankful.

After the sacrament is served, words of benediction may be said or the following:

Gracious Father, we give You praise and thanks for this Holy Communion of the body and blood of Your Son, Jesus Christ our Lord, the means of our redemption. We pray that the mercies of God may produce in us a grateful heart that finds expression through holy living and perfect love to God and to people. Through Jesus Christ our Lord. Amen.

Matrimony

CHRISTIAN MARRIAGE

CHRISTIAN MARRIAGE

Christian marriage is a sacred and public covenant between a man and a woman in the presence of God. In the Church of the Nazarene, the marriage ceremony is administered by an elder or, where the laws of the state do not prohibit, a district licensed minister who is a pastor. It is required that the marriage be attested by at least two witnesses and that it conform to the laws of the state and the requirements of the church.

A couple presenting themselves for marriage should be required to participate in premarital counseling. They shall give assurance to the officiating minister of their understanding of the biblical standard of the permanence and inviolability of the marriage covenant.

The service of Christian marriage should be conducted as a service of the worship of God and may include the reading and proclamation of the Word and music that is appropriate to Christian worship.

Holy Communion may or may not be celebrated. In services where it is desired, its meaning should be made clear. Given the meaning and significance of Holy Communion, not only should the elements be served to the bride and groom, but also the congregation should be invited to participate. There should be no pressure that would embarrass anyone present who for whatever reason does not choose to receive the elements.

The decision to perform the ceremony of Christian marriage is the responsibility of the pastor, and all requirements of the state and the church shall be fulfilled. All plans for the conduct and content of the ceremony shall be approved by the pastor. Any policies and guidelines established by the congregation regarding decorations, photography, and audio or video recording of the ceremony should be communicated by the pastor or designee during consultation and preparation for the service. Decisions regarding music content and style should be made in consultation with the pastor. Music selections should be consistent with the nature of the sacred rite and reflect Christian values and customs.

Cultural or ethnic traditions consistent with the theological stance of the church may be incorporated into the service at the discretion of the pastor.

Rite One

At the day and time appointed for the solemnization of matrimony, the persons to be married—having been qualified according to the laws of the church and of the state, and by careful counsel and guidance by the minister—standing together, facing the minister, the man to the minister's left and the woman to the right, the minister shall address the congregation as follows:

DEARLY BELOVED: We are gathered together here in the sight of God, and in the presence of these witnesses, to join together this man and this woman in holy matrimony, which is an honorable estate, instituted of God in the time of man's innocency, signifying unto us the mystical union that exists between Christ and His Church. This holy estate Christ adorned and beautified with His presence and first miracle that He wrought, in

Cana of Galilee, and St. Paul commended as being honorable among all men. It is, therefore, not to be entered into unadvisedly, but reverently, discreetly, and in the fear of God.

Into this holy estate these persons present now come to be joined.

Addressing the couple to be married, the minister shall say:

_____ and _____, I require and charge you both as you stand in the presence of God, to remember that the commitment to marriage is a commitment to permanence. It is the intent of God that your marriage will be for life, and that only death will separate you.

If the vows you exchange today be kept without violation, and if you seek always to know and do the will of God, your lives will be blessed with His presence, and your home will abide in peace.

Following the charge the minister shall say unto the man:

_____, will you have this woman to be your wedded wife, to live together after God's ordinance in the holy estate of matrimony? Will you love her, comfort her, honor and keep her in sickness and in health; and forsaking all others, keep yourself only unto her, so long as you both shall live?

Response: I will.

Then shall the minister say unto the woman:

_____, will you have this man to be your wedded husband, to live together after God's ordinance in the holy estate of matrimony? Will you love, honor, and keep him, in sickness and in health; and forsaking all others, keep yourself only unto him, so long as you both shall live?

Response: I will.

Then the minister shall ask:

Who gives this woman to be married to this man?

Response (by the father, or whoever gives the bride in marriage): I do (or, Her mother and I).

Facing each other and joining right hands, the couple shall then exchange the following vows:

The man shall repeat after the minister:

I, _____, take you, _____, to be my wedded wife, to have and to hold from this day forward, for better—for worse, for richer—for poorer, in sickness and in health, to love and to cherish, till death us do part, according to God's holy ordinance; and thereto I pledge you my faith.

The woman shall repeat after the minister:

I, _____, take you, _____, to be my wedded husband, to have and to hold from this day forward, for better—for worse, for richer—for poorer, in sickness and in health, to love and to cherish, till death us do part, according to God's holy ordinance; and thereto I pledge you my faith.

If desired, a ring ceremony may be inserted at this point. The minister receives the ring from the grooms-man and, in turn, passes it to the groom. As he then places it upon the bride's finger, he shall repeat, after the minister:

This ring I give you as a token of my love and as a pledge of my constant fidelity.

Repeat for double ring ceremony.

The couple then shall kneel as the minister offers the following, or an extemporaneous prayer:

O Eternal God, Creator and Preserver of all hu-mankind, Giver of all spiritual grace, the Author of ever-lasting life, send Thy blessing upon these Thy servants, this man and this woman, whom we now bless in Thy name; that as Isaac and Rebekah lived faithfully to-gether, so these persons may surely perform and keep the vow and covenant made between them this hour and may ever remain in love and peace together, through Jesus Christ our Lord. Amen.

Then shall the minister say:

Forasmuch as this man and woman have consented together in holy wedlock, and have witnessed the same before God and this company, and have declared the same by joining of hands, I pronounce that they are husband and wife together, in the name of the Father, and of the Son, and of the Holy Spirit. Those whom God has joined together let not man put asunder. Amen.

The minister shall then add this blessing:

God, the Father, the Son, and the Holy Spirit, bless, preserve, and keep you; the Lord mercifully with His favor look upon you, and fill you with all spiritual benediction and grace. May you so live together in this life that in the world to come you may have life everlasting.

The minister may then conclude with an extemporaneous prayer and/or benediction. (427.7, *Manual,* Church of the Nazarene)

Rite Two

GATHERING

As the people gather, instrumental or vocal music may be offered. Music used should be appropriate for Christian worship.

During the entrance of the wedding party, music may be instrumental, a congregational hymn may be sung, or a psalm, canticle, or anthem may be quoted or sung. The congregation may be invited to stand. The following processional hymns in *Sing to the Lord* are suggested:

"All Glory, Laud, and Honor," 215
"Christ Is Made the Sure Foundation," 671
"Come, Thou Almighty King," 3
"Joyful, Joyful, We Adore Thee," 17

"O God, Our Help in Ages Past," 95
"Praise, My Soul, the King of Heaven," 42
"Praise to the Lord, the Almighty," 20
"We're Marching to Zion," 389

The woman and the man may enter separately or together as the processional is engaged, accompanied by members of the wedding party. The woman and the man may be escorted by representatives of their families until they have reached the front of the church. Representatives of the families may be seated at this time or may stand with the couple through the Response of the Families, then be seated.

GREETING

Pastor to the congregation:

DEAR FRIENDS: We are gathered together in the sight of God to witness and to bless the joining together of _____ and _____ in Christian marriage. The covenant of marriage was established by God in creation when He created us male and female for each other.

Christ himself affirmed the beauty and significance of marriage with His presence and first miracle at the marriage in Cana of Galilee. Its permanence and inviolability were affirmed by Paul, who spoke with reverence of marriage as a demonstration of the relationship that Christ has with His Church. It is therefore to be entered into only with the most serious and lifelong commitment to each other's good in a union of strength, sympathy, and delight.

_____ and _____ come to give themselves to one another in this holy covenant.

DECLARATION OF INTENTION

The minister says to the persons who are to marry:

I ask you now, in the presence of God and these people, to declare your intention to enter into union with one another under the Lordship of Jesus Christ, who called you to himself and who has led you each to the other.

Minister to the woman:

_____, will you have _____ to be your husband, to live together with him in the covenant of marriage? Will you love him, comfort him, honor and keep him, in sickness and in health, and forsaking all others, be faithful to him as long as you both shall live?

Woman: I will.

Minister to the man:

_____, will you have _____ to be your wife, to live together with her in the covenant of marriage? Will you love her, comfort her, honor and keep her, in sickness and in health, and forsaking all others, be faithful to her as long as you both shall live?

Man: I will.

RESPONSES OF THE FAMILY AND CONGREGATION

Minister to the family:

The marriage of _____ and _____ unites their families and creates a new one. They ask your blessing on their union.

Parents and other representatives of the families may respond in one of the following ways:

We rejoice in your love for one another, and we pray God's blessing upon you.

Or the following:

Minister: As representatives of the families of _____ and _____, do you rejoice in their union, and do you pray God's blessing upon them?

Family members:

We do.

Minister to congregation:

Will you who witness the promises _____ and _____ have made to one another do all in your power to uphold these two persons in their marriage? If so, please answer, "We will."

Congregation: We will.

PRAYER

The minister may pray extempore or may offer the following prayer:

Eternal God, Source and Creator of all things, and Fountain of all love, grant Your grace to _____ and _____. May the years ahead find them faithful to the vows they make today, and may the strength of the Holy Spirit enable them to grow together in the love, joy, and peace of our Savior Jesus Christ. Amen.

PROCLAMATION AND RESPONSE

Here a hymn, anthem, or other music may be offered and appropriate scripture may be read in preparation for proclamation.

SERMON OR READING WITNESSING TO CHRISTIAN MARRIAGE

PRAYER OF INTERCESSION FOR THE COUPLE

The minister may offer a prayer extempore, or the following may be prayed by the minister or by the congregation:

God of grace and glory, Giver and Preserver of all life, Source of mercy:

Bless and protect _____ and _____, through the power and presence of Your Holy Spirit.

May the vows they exchange be empowered by Your presence, and may the love of Christ be the source of their love for one another.

Enable them to grow in love and peace, their lives reflecting to each other the purity that finds its pattern in the love Christ has for His Church.

Grant that their lives may be filled with compassion and sensitivity to each other, and to the needs of the world around them. May their service to others be pleasing to You, and may they find joy in extending Your love and grace to others through Jesus Christ our Lord. Amen.

The Marriage

EXCHANGE OF VOWS

The man and woman face each other and join hands. The minister prompts them as necessary in exchanging these vows:

Man to woman:

In the name of God, I, _____, take you,
_____, to be my wife,
to have and to hold
from this day forward,
for better, for worse,
for richer, for poorer,
in sickness and in health,
to love and to cherish.

Death alone shall separate us.
According to God's Holy Word,
I pledge you my faith and loyalty.

Woman to man:

In the name of God, I, _____, take you,
_____, to be my husband,
to have and to hold
from this day forward,
for better, for worse,

for richer, for poorer,
in sickness and in health,
to love and to cherish.

Death alone shall separate us.
According to God's Holy Word,
I pledge you my faith and loyalty.

BLESSING AND EXCHANGE OF RINGS

The exchange of rings is optional. Where preferred, other symbols may be given instead of rings.

The minister, upon receiving the rings from the bearer, may say one of the following:

These rings are the outward and visible sign of an inward and spiritual grace, signifying to us the joining of _____ and _____ in holy marriage.

The minister may then bless the rings with an extempore prayer or the following:

Most Holy God, bless these rings *(this ring, these symbols)*. Grant that they who wear them may be faithful to each other and may be constant in their love for each other to their lives' end, through Jesus Christ our Lord. Amen.

The minister gives each ring in turn to the couple. While placing the ring on the third finger of the recipient's left hand, the giver may say (prompted by the minister):

_____, I give you this *ring* as a symbol of my
    love,
  and with all that I am and all that I have,
I commit myself to you;
    in the name of the Father and of the Son and of
       the Holy Spirit. Amen.

BLESSING OF THE MARRIAGE

The husband and wife may kneel as the minister prays:

O Eternal God, You have so honored the covenant
of marriage that in it is found the demonstration of the
covenant between Christ and His Church. You have so
constituted it that it is entered into for as long as this
life shall last.

_____ and _____ entered this covenant willingly with the purpose that their lives may grow in god-
liness and love, and that their home shall be a haven of
grace and peace. May they keep their covenant of love
for one another as faithfully as You have kept Your
covenant of love with us. And may the power of Your
Holy Spirit empower them for keeping their promises in
all the years to come. Amen.

DECLARATION OF MARRIAGE

The husband and wife join hands. The minister may
place a hand on their joined hands.

Now that _____ and _____ have given

77

themselves to each other through the exchange of vows, by the joining of hands, and by the giving and receiving of rings, I pronounce that they are husband and wife together, in the name of the Father and of the Son and of the Holy Spirit. Those whom God has joined together in marriage, let no one ever separate. Amen.

> If Holy Communion is to be celebrated, the service continues with the Thanksgiving and with the elements offered to all the congregation. The service order may follow the order of service found in this handbook, "The Sacrament of the Lord's Supper" Rites One and Two, or as indicated in the following section. A marriage ceremony in which Holy Communion is celebrated may best be facilitated by providing a written order of worship for the congregation.

> If Holy Communion is not to be celebrated, the service continues with the following Prayer of Thanksgiving:

Most gracious God, Creator and Preserver of all people, we give You thanks for Your love and tenderness.

You have made us a covenant people through our Savior Jesus Christ and have demonstrated Your grace in bringing together these two people whose love we celebrate this day.

May Christ's love purify their love for each other, and may His presence keep them sensitive to the needs of the other.

Let their love be a demonstration of Your love to the world around them, and honor their service to others as service to You.

Bless them in their work and in their companionship; in their waking and in their sleeping; in their sorrows and in their joys; in their living and in their dying.

At last, may their lives be crowned by the approval You grant them, that they may join us all at that table where Your saints feast forever in Your heavenly home; through Jesus Christ our Lord, who with You and the Holy Spirit lives and reigns, one God, for ever and ever. Amen.

THANKSGIVING AND COMMUNION

(See instructions for serving Holy Communion in this handbook.)

Minister: The Lord be with you.

People: And also with you.

Minister: Lift up your hearts.

People: We lift them to the Lord.

Minister: Let us give thanks to the Lord our God.

People: It is right to give Him thanks and praise.

It is right, and a good and joyful thing, always and everywhere to give thanks to You, Father Almighty, Creator of heaven and earth.

Because in the love of wife and husband, You have

given us an image of the heavenly Jerusalem, adorned as a bride for her bridegroom, Your Son Jesus Christ our Lord; who loves her and gave himself for her, that He might make the whole creation new.

And so, with Your people on earth and all the company of heaven, we praise Your name and say,

"Holy, holy, holy Lord, God of power and might, heaven and earth are full of Your glory. Hosanna in the highest. Blessed is he who comes in the name of the Lord. Hosanna in the highest."

Holy are You, and blessed is Your Son Jesus Christ, whom You sent in the fullness of time to be a light to the world. In the new covenant established in His blood is the image for the covenant love of husband and wife.

On the night in which He gave himself for us, He took bread, gave thanks to You, broke the bread, gave it to His disciples, and said: "Take, eat: this is my body, which is broken for you: this do in remembrance of me" (1 Cor. 11:24).

When the supper was ended, He took the cup, gave thanks to You, gave it to His disciples, and said: "Drink from it, all of you. This is my blood of the covenant, which is poured out for many for the forgiveness of sins" (Matt. 26:27-28, NIV). "Do this, whenever you drink it, in remembrance of me" (1 Cor. 11:25, NIV).

And so, in remembrance of these Your mighty acts in Jesus Christ, we offer ourselves in praise and thanksgiving as a holy and living sacrifice, in union with Christ's offering for us, as we proclaim the mystery of faith.

"Christ has died, Christ is risen, Christ will come again."

Pour out Your Holy Spirit on us, gathered here, and on these gifts of bread and wine. Make them be for us the body and blood of Christ, that we may be for the world the Body of Christ, redeemed by His blood.

Bless _____ and _____ with Your Holy Spirit. May their love reflect the love Christ has for us, a love that is pure and strong.

By Your Spirit make them one with Christ, one with each other, and one in ministry to all the world, until Christ comes in final victory and we, with them, feast at His heavenly banquet.

Through Your Son Jesus Christ, with the Holy Spirit in Your holy Church, all honor and glory is Yours, Almighty Father, now and forever. Amen.

THE LORD'S PRAYER

Minister: And now, with these whom God has united in marriage, let us pray:

"Our Father, who art in heaven, hallowed be thy name. Thy kingdom come, thy will be done, on earth as it is in heaven. Give us this day our daily bread. And forgive us our trespasses, as we forgive those who trespass against us. And lead us not into temptation, but deliver us from evil. For thine is the kingdom and the power and the glory forever. Amen" (see Matt. 6:9-13).

BREAKING THE BREAD

The minister, standing behind the Lord's table facing the congregation, breaks the bread and then lifts the cup in silence or with appropriate words.

COMMUNION

The bread and wine are given to the congregation with appropriate words being exchanged. The husband and wife may assist in the distribution.

The body of Christ, given for you. Amen.

The blood of Christ, given for you. Amen.

While the bread and wine are given, the congregation may sing hymns, or there may be appropriate vocal or instrumental music.

When all have received, the Lord's table is put in order.

The minister may then offer prayer:

God of mercy and love,

You have brought _____ and _____ together along with this company of friends and family. We have feasted at Your table and rejoice in Your love.

Grant that these two servants of Yours may grow in love, in wisdom, and in spiritual strength. Crown their home with blessing and peace. May their living here please You and serve Your kingdom.

Through Jesus Christ our Lord. Amen.

BLESSING AND DISMISSAL

Minister to husband and wife:

God grant you the peace of Christ, the joy of service, and the wisdom of years. May His peace fill your home and His grace guide your going. Go to serve God and your neighbor in all that you do.

Minister to people:

Bear witness to the love of God in your world, and be filled with His Spirit in your words and your doing. The love of God, the grace of the Lord Jesus Christ, and the presence of the Holy Spirit be with you all. Amen.

The couple may greet each other with a kiss and be greeted by the pastor, after which greetings may be exchanged through the congregation.

A hymn may be sung or instrumental music played as the couple, the wedding party, and the people leave.

Rite Three

The following ceremony provides an alternative to the more frequently used ceremonies. Drawn from a variety of resources, it provides some options that may be utilized in planning a ceremony that highlights the centrality of worship in the rituals of the church.

GATHERING

While the people are gathering, music appropriate for Christian worship is played, utilizing vocal or instrumental music. During the Gathering, guests and family members are seated, and candles are lighted.

After guests and family are seated, the entrance of the wedding party is accompanied by a hymn, by an anthem, or by other appropriate music. The entrance of the grandparents and parents of the bride and groom signifies the beginning of the ceremony. Their order of entry is as follows: the groom's grandparents, the bride's grandparents, the groom's parents, the bride's mother.

After the grandparents and parents are seated, the order of entry of the wedding party is typically as follows: the ushers or groomsmen, bridesmaids, maid (unmarried woman)/matron (married woman) of honor, ring bearer(s), and flower girl(s).

The woman and the man, entering separately or together, now come forward with other members of the wedding party. The woman and the man may be escorted by representatives of their families (traditionally, the groom by his father or best man, and the bride by her father or other male family member) until they have reached the front of the church or through the Response of the Families, at which time the escort(s) (usually the bride's escort) is seated. The couple facing the minister, the minister facing the congregation, the ceremony continues.

GREETINGS

DEAR FRIENDS: We have come together in the presence of God to witness and to bless the joining of _____ and _____ in Christian marriage.

The covenant of marriage was established by God in creation and has been blessed through the ages by the people of God. Our Lord Jesus Christ blessed this manner of life with words of affirmation and instruction, and His presence and first miracle, at a marriage in Cana of Galilee.

Christian marriage signifies to us the beauty and mystery of the union that Christ has with His Church, and the Scripture commends it to be honored among all people.

The union of husband and wife in heart, body, and mind is intended by God for their mutual joy; for the help and comfort given each other in all seasons and conditions in life; and when God so provides, for the procreation of children and their nurture and training in the knowledge and love of God in Christ.

Christian marriage is therefore of great significance. It is not to be entered with haste or lack of careful thought and prayer but reverently, deliberately, and in careful accord with the purposes for which it is intended by God.

THE CHARGE TO THE MAN AND THE WOMAN

_____ and _____, as you stand before this gathered company of friends and family, and as you present yourselves to God, I charge you to remember that you enter into a covenant with each other that is patterned after the covenant of faithfulness God has established with us.

Your marriage is to be the object of your best endeavors. So live in loyalty and faithfulness to each other that your home becomes eloquent testimony to the character of your relationship with the Lord Jesus Christ. May He be the acknowledged Witness to your words and deeds, your thoughts and attitudes. May the quality of your life together be measured by the depth of your love for Him.

THE DECLARATION OF INTENT

The minister shall address the man as follows:

Will you, _____, take _____ to be your wife; and will you now promise, in the presence of God and before these gathered witnesses, to be a loving, faithful, and loyal husband to her, whatever may come, until God shall separate you by death?

The man shall answer:

I will.

The minister shall then address the woman as follows:

Will you, _____, take _____ to be your husband; and will you now promise, in the presence of God and before these gathered witnesses, to be a loving, faithful, and loyal wife to him, whatever may come, until God shall separate you by death?

The woman shall answer:

I will.

BLESSING OF THE COUPLE BY THE PARENTS OR FAMILIES

The minister may address the families of the bride and groom as follows:

_____, _____ [names of families' members], do you give your blessing to _____ and _____ and promise to do everything in your power to uphold them in their marriage?

The families may respond:

We rejoice in your union and pray God's blessing upon your home.

BLESSING OF THE COUPLE BY THE CONGREGATION

The minister may address the congregation as follows:

Dear friends of _____ and _____: You have come to witness this exchange of vows. Will you do all in your power to support this marriage now and in the years to come? If so, please answer, "We will."

The congregation shall answer:

We will.

PRAYER FOR ILLUMINATION

The minister may pray extemporaneously or pray the following:

O God of light and understanding, You show us the way, the truth, and the life. You sustain us with Your Holy Spirit. We take joy in Your presence with us and pray for Your guidance and illumination as we hear Your Word. May _____ and _____ find strength in this moment of openness to You. Through Jesus Christ our Lord. Amen.

READING FROM SCRIPTURE

One or more scripture passages are read.

HOMILY

Suggested homilies are included in the *Manual* appendix and may serve as models for developing of a homily or may be used as printed.

Following the homily, an appropriate hymn or other response may be used.

The Marriage

EXCHANGE OF VOWS

The woman and the man face each other and join hands. The minister may prompt them in the repeating of the vows to one another.

The man shall say to the woman:

I, _____, receive you, _____, as a gift
  from God,
  to be my lifelong companion.
I will love you through laughter and tears,
  through health and sickness,
  in plenty and in want,
  at work and at play.
I will love you constantly and with the deepest
  loyalty.

I will prayerfully seek your joy and happiness
  throughout our lives. Amen.

The woman shall say to the man:

I, _____, receive you, _____, as a gift
  from God,
  to be my lifelong companion.
I will love you through laughter and tears,
  through health and sickness,
  in plenty and in want,
  at work and at play.
I will love you constantly and with the deepest
  loyalty.
I will prayerfully seek your joy and happiness
  throughout our lives. Amen.

BLESSING AND EXCHANGE OF RINGS

The exchange of rings is optional. Other symbols may
be given in addition to or instead of rings.

The minister may say one of the following:

Most gracious God, in the time of Noah, You gave
the rainbow as a sign of promise. Bless these symbols
that they may also be signs of promises fulfilled in the
lives of these servants of Yours, through Jesus Christ our
Lord. Amen.

While placing the ring on the third finger of the recipient's left hand, the giver may say the following:

_____, I give you this ring as a sign of my vow,

and with all that I am, and all that I have, I honor you; in the name of the Father and of the Son and of the Holy Spirit. Amen.

UNITY CANDLE

The lighting of a unity candle is a recently developed tradition in the wedding service. It is intended to symbolize the oneness that characterizes Christian marriage.

When a unity candle is desired, the two side candles, representing the husband and wife, are lighted early in the service, often by the mothers of the bride and groom while the family is being seated at the beginning of the service.

The center candle is lighted by the bride and groom after the exchange of vows and the exchange of rings. The side candles remain lighted to symbolize that each partner retains his or her personal identity while the two are united as husband and wife.

During the lighting of the unity candle, music may be played or sung.

An explanation of the symbolism of the candle may be given by the minister prior to the lighting. The minister may read one of the following:

The unity candle symbolizes that _____ and _____ are joined together as one flesh. They have become one and are intended to treat each other as if the other were a part of their own flesh.

The love that is characterized by this unity is best described by the words of Ruth to Naomi in the Old Testament: "Do not press me to leave you or to turn back from following you! Where you go, I will go; where you lodge, I will lodge; your people shall be my people, and your God my God. Where you die, I will die—there will I be buried" (Ruth 1:16-17, NRSV).

Or:

"Then the man said, 'This at last is bone of my bones and flesh of my flesh; this one shall be called Woman, for out of Man this one was taken.' Therefore a man leaves his father and his mother and clings to his wife, and they become one flesh" (Gen. 2:23-24, NRSV).

DECLARATION OF MARRIAGE

The wife and husband join hands and face the minister. The minister may place a hand on their joined hands.

Pastor to bride and groom:

You have declared your vows and given symbols of your love before God and this congregation. May God confirm your covenant and fill you both with His grace.

The couple may turn and face the congregation.

Pastor to people:

Now that _____ and _____ have given themselves to each other by solemn vows, with the joining of hands, (and the giving and receiving of rings,) I announce to you that they are husband and wife; in the name of the Father and of the Son and of the Holy Spirit.

Those whom God has joined together, let no one ever separate.

The congregation may be invited to stand while a doxology or other appropriate hymn is sung.

THE BLESSING OF THE MARRIAGE

The groom and bride may kneel as the minister prays:

Eternal God, You have blessed the covenant of Christian marriage, investing in it the symbolism of the union that exists between Christ and His Church. On this holy union between _____ and _____ grant Your blessing and peace. May the testimony of their lives give joy to You, and may they find Your Holy Spirit empowering them to grow in love and likeness to Christ. May their home be a place of refuge and happiness for them both, and may the joy You take in them be seen in the blessings You bestow upon them. Through Jesus Christ our Lord. Amen.

If Holy Communion is to be celebrated, the congregation is invited to participate with the wedding party as the service continues with the thanksgiving and Communion. (See the Sacrament of the Lord's Supper section of this handbook.)

If Holy Communion is not to be celebrated, the service continues with a prayer of thanksgiving given extemporaneously by the minister, or the following prayer may be read:

Gracious Father, accept our thanks for Your making us a covenant people through Jesus Christ our Lord. And thank You for blessing _____ and _____ in the exchange of their vows of love and loyalty this day.

Grant that their love for each other may reflect the love of Christ for us, and may that love grow in them daily.

Honor their home with Your presence, and preserve their commitments with Your strength.

Bless their work and their service, and may they know the peace and prosperity both desire, which shall yield to You for Your purposes.

May their living be of such joy to You that they shall finally stand before You with assurance and be able to sit at the table with Your saints from all ages. Through Jesus Christ our Lord, who with You and the Holy Spirit lives and reigns for ever and ever. Amen.

DISMISSAL WITH BLESSING

Here a song or hymn may be sung.

Minister to bride and groom:

God the Father bless you and preserve you; Christ

the Lord honor your vows with His peace; God the Holy Spirit fill you with His love, as you seek His will and do it.

Minister to congregation:

Bear witness to the love of God in this world, so that those to whom love is a stranger will find it in your generous friends. The grace of the Lord Jesus Christ and the love of God and the communion of the Holy Spirit be with you all. Amen.

The couple may greet each other with a kiss. If desired, the minister may introduce the couple to the congregation. A hymn may be sung or instrumental music may be played as the couple, the wedding party, and the people leave.

SUBSEQUENT MARRIAGE

On occasion, ministers are asked to solemnize the marriage of persons who, as a result of death or divorce, are entering a subsequent marriage. If after careful counsel and in following the guidelines of the *Manual* a minister believes that the marriage fulfills the best of God's plan for the couple, the marriage should address the needs of any children who will live in the home. If desired, the children may be asked to participate in the ceremony, and the following may serve as a model for their participation in a commitment to growth, stability, and peace in the home.

The minister may address the children as follows:

Your parents have discovered in one another a deep and abiding love. They have prayerfully sought the will of God for themselves and for you and desire that each of you be a vital part of this family that God has brought together. They have committed themselves to one another in marriage, believing it is best for them and for you.

Will you commit yourselves to seek to be a family that learns to love one another as Christ loves us? (Where other living parents exist, the following may be included if the couple desires to do so:) While there are other parents for whom you have, and should have, a deep and abiding love, will you seek to encourage and support your father (mother) in this marriage and allow God to bless this home with His grace and peace?

If, with God's help, you will do this, please answer, "I will."

Children: I will.

HOMILY:

Scripture: 1 Cor. 13

_____ and _____, those are words of great power and significance for you today. And as we, your family and friends, join you in the celebration of your marriage vows, we could wish for the two of you nothing greater than that your love would be characterized by the qualities described in that passage of Holy Scripture.

The apostle Paul gives us a powerful model for married love in these verses. Love's definition is seen in its most compelling description. You see, you must always remember that love is not a feeling you have; love is something you do! Oh, I am not saying you do not or should not feel deeply about your love and about the one you love. And the love each of you feels for the other is moving and deep. There is an emotional content to love that is very satisfying. But Paul reminds us here that when the emotional tone in your lives and in your marriage tends to ebb and flow, as it will from time to time, loving deeds and intentions must still be the foundation of your relationship.

Hear these words again: "Love is patient; love is kind; love is not . . . boastful . . . or rude. It does not insist on its own way; it is not irritable or resentful. . . . It bears all things," believes all the best of its object, and is enduringly hopeful (NRSV). Love, you see, is not determined by how you feel. It is the choice you make toward your beloved one.

In your love, make room for forgiveness. And in your forgiveness, make room for growth. Each of you must learn to forgive readily and to seek forgiveness readily. It will not always be easy, and it must never be one-sided. You will have plenty of reasons for forgiveness, but hopefully, each occasion will also be an occasion for growth, as persons and as a couple, in your relationship with each other and in your relationship with Christ. That is what Paul is saying to us.

Those are strong words! And they would be impossible to understand were it not that each of you has come to know, very personally, the One who is the Source of such love. The apostle Paul himself knew what you know as well. Love like that is patterned after and made possible only by Jesus Christ. The only way you can hope to offer to each other a love as pure and meaningful as that is when you know and understand the Source of that love. You cannot produce it on your own. It is the love of God himself poured into your life by the Holy Spirit, through Jesus Christ. It is yours when you have allowed Him to become Lord of life for each of you as persons and for you as a couple, as husband and wife.

My prayer for you both is that you will continue to allow this love to find its source, not in your ability to produce it, but in His ability to provide it in you and through you.

And remember this: Neither of you will be able to find in each other the ultimate source of love and meaning. That each of you must find only in Jesus Christ. But once you find your meaning and love in Him, you will be able to give love and meaning to the other. Find your ultimate fulfillment in Christ, and you will then be able to give fulfillment to each other.

_____ and _____, we, all of us who are

here with you today, wish for you the very best of God's blessings. May your lives be filled with love as they are filled with Christ.

The Funeral Service

THE BURIAL OF THE DEAD

THE BURIAL OF THE DEAD

Among the most significant responsibilities of a pastor is care for the dying, the burial of the dead, and ministry to the grieving. While this is a time of deep emotion for all involved, both family and friends, it is also a time for the reaffirmation of the hope that Christian believers have in light of the resurrection of Christ.

"The liturgy for the dead is an Easter liturgy," says the Book of Common Prayer. "It finds all its meaning in the resurrection. Because Jesus was raised from the dead, we, too, shall be raised."[12]

This does not mean that human grief is somehow inappropriate or unchristian. The loss of a loved one or friend to death is a parting that brings real pain. We must acknowledge such grief and minister the tender consolations of Christ to those who mourn.

But the pastor must also remind believers of the promise of the resurrection. The memorial or funeral service must always contain a note of hope and confidence. While we sorrow, we do not sorrow as those who have no hope (1 Thess. 4:13), but even in our grief, we look forward to a day of resurrection (v. 14).

In the variety of settings in which we minister, there is no single standard form of funeral order. While the traditions vary from place to place, there are some protocols that are appropriate to a Christian funeral that may provide a recommended order for use on such occasions.

It is especially appropriate that a Christian's funeral be held in the church. It is in the sanctuary that the message of hope may sound its most certain note. It is in the death and resurrection of Christ, the head of the Church, that the Christian community finds it central reason for existence. That certainty and hope are most needed by those who mourn and can best be ministered in the context where that hope is visibly represented in the symbols of cross, altar, and table.

Below is a ritual for the funeral that can be modified for believers, nonbelievers, or children.

The Funeral Service

DEARLY BELOVED: We are gathered today to pay our final tribute of respect to that which was mortal of our deceased loved one and friend. To you members of the family who mourn your loss, we especially offer our deep and sincere sympathy. May we share with you the comfort afforded by God's Word for such a time as this:

"Do not let your hearts be troubled. Trust in God; trust also in me. In my Father's house are many rooms; if it were not so, I would have told you. I am going there to prepare a place for you. And if I go and prepare a place for you, I will come back and take you to be with me that you also may be where I am" (John 14:1-3, NIV).

"Jesus said to her, 'I am the resurrection and the life. He who believes in me will live, even though he dies; and whoever lives and believes in me will never die. Do you believe this?'" (John 11:25-26, NIV).

INVOCATION

In the minister's own words or the following:

Almighty God, our Heavenly Father, we come into this sanctuary of sorrow, realizing our utter dependence upon Thee. We know Thou dost love us and canst turn even the shadow of death into the light of morning. Help us now to wait before Thee with reverent and submissive hearts.

Thou art our Refuge and Strength, O God—a very present Help in time of trouble. Grant unto us Thy abundant mercy. May those who mourn today find comfort and healing balm in Thy sustaining grace. We humbly bring these petitions in the name of our Lord Jesus Christ. Amen.

A Hymn or Special Song

Selections of Scripture

"Praise be to the God and Father of our Lord Jesus Christ! In his great mercy he has given us new birth into a living hope through the resurrection of Jesus Christ from the dead, and into an inheritance that can never perish, spoil or fade—kept in heaven for you, who through faith are shielded by God's power until the coming of the salvation that is ready to be revealed in the last time. In this you greatly rejoice, though now for a little while you may have had to suffer grief in all kinds of trials. These have come so that your faith—of greater worth than gold, which perishes even though refined by fire—may be proved genuine and may result in praise, glory and honor when Jesus Christ is revealed. Though you have not seen him, you love him; and even though you do not see him now, you believe in him and are filled with an inexpressible and glorious joy, for you are receiving the goal of your faith, the salvation of your souls" (1 Pet. 1:3-9, NIV).

(Other passages that might be used are: Matt. 5:3-4, 6, 8; Pss. 27:3-5, 11, 13-14; 46:1-6, 10-11.)

MESSAGE

A HYMN OR SPECIAL SONG

CLOSING PRAYER

* * *

AT THE GRAVESIDE

When the people have assembled, the minister may read any or all of the following scriptures:

"I know that my Redeemer lives, and that in the end he will stand upon the earth. And after my skin has been destroyed, yet in my flesh I will see God; I myself will see him with my own eyes—I, and not another" (Job 19:25-27, NIV).

"Listen, I tell you a mystery: We will not all sleep, but we will all be changed—in a flash, in the twinkling of an eye, at the last trumpet. For the trumpet will sound, the dead will be raised imperishable, and we will be changed. . . . Then the saying that is written will come true: 'Death has been swallowed up in victory. Where,

O death, is your victory? Where, O death, is your sting?'
The sting of death is sin, and the power of sin is the law.
But thanks be to God! He gives us the victory through
our Lord Jesus Christ.

"Therefore, my dear brothers, stand firm. Let nothing move you. Always give yourselves fully to the work
of the Lord, because you know that your labor in the
Lord is not in vain" (1 Cor. 15:51-52, 54-58, NIV).

"Then I heard a voice from heaven say, 'Write:
Blessed are the dead who die in the Lord from now on.'
'Yes,' says the Spirit, 'they will rest from their labor, for
their deeds will follow them'" (Rev. 14:13, NIV).

The minister shall then read one of the following committal statements:

For a Believer:

Forasmuch as the spirit of our departed loved one
has returned to God, who gave it, we therefore tenderly
commit his (her) body to the grave in sure trust and certain hope of the resurrection of the dead and the life of
the world to come, through our Lord Jesus Christ, who
shall give to us new bodies like unto His glorious body.
"Blessed are the dead which die in the Lord."

For a Nonbeliever:

We have come now to commit the body of our departed friend to its kindred dust. The spirit we leave
with God, for we know the merciful Judge of all the

earth will do right. Let us who remain dedicate ourselves anew to live in the fear and love of God, so that we may obtain an abundant entrance into the heavenly Kingdom.

For a Child:

In the sure and certain hope of the resurrection to eternal life through our Lord Jesus Christ, we commit the body of this child to the grave. And as Jesus, during His earthly life, took the children into His arms and blessed them, may He receive this dear one unto himself, for, as He said, "The kingdom of heaven belongs to such as these" (Matt. 19:14, NIV).

PRAYER

Our Heavenly Father, God of all mercy, we look to Thee in this moment of sorrow and bereavement. Comfort these dear ones whose hearts are heavy and sad. Wilt Thou be with them, sustain and guide them in the days to come. Grant, O Lord, that they may love and serve Thee and obtain the fullness of Thy promises in the world to come.

"May the God of peace, who through the blood of the eternal covenant brought back from the dead our Lord Jesus, that great Shepherd of the sheep, equip you with everything good for doing his will, and may he work in us what is pleasing to him, through Jesus Christ, to whom be glory for ever and ever. Amen" (Heb. 13:20-21, NIV).

Alternate Order of Burial

In those situations where it is not possible or preferable to use the order found in the preceding ritual, the following order for burial may serve as a guide for the minister and those who are responsible for the conduct of the service.

THE BODY IS RECEIVED

The minister or celebrant may meet the body and conduct it into the church or chapel. It may also be in place before the congregation arrives for the service.

It is appropriate for the casket to be closed prior to the conduct of the service and to remain closed for burial.

SELECTED PASSAGES OF SCRIPTURE MAY BE READ

The passages of Scripture may express the grief and anguish of loss often found in the Psalms or other similar passages.

A HYMN MAY BE SUNG

PRAYER IS OFFERED FOR THOSE WHO MOURN

ONE OR MORE ADDITIONAL PASSAGES OF SCRIPTURE MAY BE READ

Here the passages of hope and consolation may be read.

A HOMILY OR BRIEF MESSAGE MAY FOLLOW THE READINGS

PRAYER IS OFFERED IN MEMORY OF THE DECEASED AND ON BEHALF OF THOSE WHO GRIEVE

THE DECEASED IS COMMENDED TO GOD, AND THE BODY IS COMMITTED TO ITS RESTING PLACE

The committal may take place either where the preceding service has been held or at the graveside.

Following the service of committal, ministry to the family and friends of the deceased is one of the most important duties of the pastor. This will require time spent with the family and reassurances of God's gracious promise of comfort and restoration.

Installation Services

INSTALLATION OF PASTOR

INSTALLATION OF OFFICERS

INSTALLATION OF PASTOR

The installation of a pastor is a sacred and significant event in the life of a congregation and in the life of the pastor. The process of searching for, nominating, electing, and installing a pastor offers opportunity for the congregation to reexamine its mission, reaffirm its core values, and anticipate the continuing leadership of the Holy Spirit in the ministry of the church to its community.

The opportunity to celebrate the beginning of a new relationship will strengthen the ties between pastor and people and should receive the highest attention by all concerned.

The district superintendent should be given opportunity to participate in the service, where possible, and may wish to be involved in the design of the service. Local leaders should plan the service well, using it as an opportunity to involve the widest possible number of people in relating to and installing the pastor as shepherd and overseer of the flock of God.

The following suggested order of service and ritual is designed to provide for meaningful interaction between platform leaders, the pastor, and the congregation. Careful attention should be given to every element of the service and adequate time given to prepare a meaningful and affirming service.

PRELUDE

PROCESSIONAL

PRAISE

Various hymns may be used to celebrate the leadership and faithfulness of God.

PRAYER

CREED

The Apostles' Creed may be read in unison at this place in the service.

INSTALLATION OF PASTOR

Ceremony of Installation

PART I: INTRODUCTION (District Superintendent)

For 20 centuries now, in every generation, the Church has set aside some of her members for special training and preparation, ordaining them to serve as clergy. She elects them to positions of responsibility, not privilege. They are to serve the needs of the Church. These ministers give up their lives, so to speak, for their lives are not their own; they serve if and when and where and in the capacities that the Church invites them to serve. They are the servants of God. The Early Church referred to them with words that meant "table waiter," "under rower" (oarsman in a large ship), "slave," "priestly servant," and "shepherd." The Church ordains only those whom she believes God has called to such service.

District Superintendent to New Pastor: Will you accept the charge to be the spiritual leader of this flock?

Pastor: I will.

District Superintendent to Congregation: Will you,

the members of this church, accept, support, and uphold Rev. _____ as your pastor?

Congregation: We will.

PART II: INVITATION AND COVENANT FOR THE CHURCH

1. *A Sunday School Teacher*

Accept this Bible and be among us "a man (woman) of one book," as Mr. Wesley said, be in this place one who proclaims the Word.

2. *Member of Board of Stewards*

Receive this vessel of water, the water of baptism. Be among us an evangelist who brings many to the knowledge of Jesus Christ as Lord and Savior, and to the affirmation of faith pronounced by the baptismal water.

3. *Sanctuary Choir President*

Receive this hymnal and be among us a leading worshiper at the foot of the Cross, that we may worthily magnify the name of God and our Savior, Jesus Christ.

4. *A Young Family*

Receive this directory containing a list of all our families. We are all your people. Pray for us, and be a priest and pastor among us that we might be acceptable to the Lord.

5. *Member of Board of Stewards*

Receive this oil, and be a healer and reconciler among us and a model of spiritual leadership to those of us training for ministry.

6. *A Senior Couple*

Accept this *Manual of the Church of the Nazarene* and the duty of teaching and discipling this people, reminding us that we are not only Christians but also Nazarene Christians.

7. *The District Superintendent*

Take this bread and cup and with it the authority to administer in Christ's stead the sacrament of Holy Communion among this people.

COVENANTAL LITANY

Congregation led by secretary of the church board. Congregation standing.

Leader: Will you affirm that you believe that this pastor and this church are to be workers together in the providence of God?

People: This we do believe and affirm.

Leader: Will you support this pastor with respect, loyalty, love, and fervent prayer?

People: This we will do with God's help.

Leader: Will you receive the pastor's family members as members of our own family of faith, and love and pray for them as our own?

People: This we will do with God's help.

Leader: Will you give sacrificially of your means so

that this pastor can be relieved of the temporal cares of this life so that he (she) may give his (her) full attention "to prayer, and to the ministry of the word" (Acts 6:4)?

People: This we will do with God's help.

Leader: Will you respond to pastoral leadership by vigorous participation in the congregational life of this church as it carries out its fourfold mission of worship, evangelism, nurture, and service?

People: This we will do with God's help.

Reading of the Word

Congregation seated.

A Church Board Member: "Here is my servant, whom I uphold, my chosen one in whom I delight; I will put my Spirit on him and he will bring justice to the nations. He will not shout or cry out, or raise his voice in the streets. A bruised reed he will not break, and a smoldering wick he will not snuff out. In faithfulness he will bring forth justice; he will not falter or be discouraged till he establishes justice on earth. In his law the islands will put their hope" (Isa. 42:1-4, NIV).

A Church Board Member: "This is what God the LORD says—he who created the heavens and stretched them out, who spread out the earth and all that comes out of it, who gives breath to its people, and life to those who walk on it: 'I, the LORD, have called you in righteousness; I will take hold of your hand. I will keep you and will make you to be a covenant for the people and a light for the Gentiles, to open eyes that are blind, to free captives from prison and to release from the dungeon those who sit in darkness'" (Isa. 42:5-7, NIV).

A Sunday School Teacher: "To each one of us grace was given according to the measure of Christ's gift. . . .

"He Himself gave some to be apostles, some prophets, some evangelists, and some pastors and teachers, for the equipping of the saints for the work of ministry, for the edifying of the body of Christ."

A Church Member: "Till we all come to the unity of the faith and the knowledge of the Son of God."

A Church Member: "To a perfect man, to the measure of the stature of the fullness of Christ."

A Church Member: "That we . . . speaking the truth in love, may grow up in all things into Him who is the head—Christ."

Congregation: "From whom the whole body, joined and knit together by what every joint supplies, according to the effective working by which every part does its share, causes growth of the body for the edifying of itself in love" (Eph. 4:7, 11-16, NKJV).

PART III: THE PASTOR'S COVENANT:

In response to the gracious call of God and in gratitude for the confidence you have expressed in me, I receive these symbols of pastoral leadership.

I pledge to you a stewardship of these resources and covenant with you to make ours a living, efficient church:

—a church in which sermon and sacrament are based strongly on the Word and enlivened with the dynamic presence of the Holy Spirit

—a church with the atmospheric expectation of conversions

—a church where the tempted are environed with victory

—a church where the redeemed are enabled to see their larger need of Christ in cleansing fullness

—a church where the particular consolations of God are given to the afflicted

—a church where Christian men and women begin even on earth to be an authentic Christian community

—a church that constantly bears toward the whole world with sacrifice in its heart and conquest in its purpose

I pledge to you a stewardship of my responsibilities as pastor:

—to live before you with integrity and Christian simplicity

—to responsibly administer the affairs of the church

in consultation and cooperation with the church board, the church staff, and the people of the congregation as we carry out "the work of the ministry, for the edifying of the body of Christ" (Eph. 4:12)

—to lead you in worship as a worshiping leader, developing a careful regimen of study, prayer, reflection, and preparation, for the purposes of personal growth and ministry

—to encourage you, comfort you, instruct and challenge you, by the preaching of the Word and the administration of the sacraments

—to seek always and in all appropriate ways to expand the borders of the kingdom of God, cooperating with the district and general Church of the Nazarene in fulfilling a worldwide agenda

—to live my family role responsibly, giving to each member the care and love due him (her) as a gift of God to me

—to listen carefully to you, care deeply for you, work closely with you, and pray daily for you, that we may "grow up in all things into Him who is the head—Christ" (Eph. 4:15)

—to be a servant-leader, after the example of Christ

PART IV: CHARGE TO PASTOR AND CHURCH

District Superintendent to the Pastor: Having committed yourself to this work, I charge you to care alike for the young and old, strong and weak, rich and poor. By your words and by your life proclaim the gospel of Jesus Christ.

District Superintendent to the Congregation: Since you have willingly and prayerfully called Pastor _____ to work among you, I charge you to willingly and prayerfully support, cooperate, and work together with him (her) in the name of Jesus Christ, whom you both serve.

PART V: MUTUAL COVENANT BETWEEN PASTOR AND PEOPLE

Pastor and people read in unison:

Congregation standing.

- We shall strive to cooperatively create and sustain an effective ministry that will renew and strengthen each member of this community of faith.
- We shall actively seek and welcome into membership all persons without regard to their economic or social status, race, or nationality.
- We shall accept our responsibility for moral and spiritual development in our community, living by Christian standards of good citizenship.
- We shall work together with other churches and denominations in our community for the advance-

ment of Christ's kingdom whenever we have the opportunity to do so.

- We shall periodically evaluate our church's fellowship and ministry in light of our mission.
- If problems present barriers to the mutual effectiveness of pastor and congregation, we shall cooperatively pray, faithfully communicate, and work in love to find solutions in the spirit of Christian understanding.
- We shall work to insure that our church appropriately relates itself to the mission, institutions, and doctrines of the Church of the Nazarene and the redemptive mission of Christ in our community, nation, and the world. Amen.

District Superintendent: By the power invested in me as superintendent of the _____ District of the Church of the Nazarene, I announce to you that having committed themselves to mutual covenants, Pastor _____ and the _____ Church of the Nazarene have entered a new and solemn relationship, that of pastor and people. Please greet your new senior pastor.

PRAISE SONG: "God's Faithfulness"

Introduction of New Family by District Superintendent

OFFERTORY

DOXOLOGY

MINISTRY IN MUSIC

MESSAGE

RESPONSE

INVITATION TO RECEPTION

PRAYER

BENEDICTION

INSTALLATION OF OFFICERS

Following the singing of an appropriate hymn, let the secretary read the names and positions of the officers to be installed. These may come forward and stand at the altar of the church, facing the minister. A covenant card (see pages 123-24) should be provided for each. The minister shall then say:

Recognizing God's method of setting apart certain workers for specific areas of Christian service, we come to this moment of installation of these officers (and/or teachers) who have been duly chosen to serve in our church for the ensuing year. Let us consider God's instructions to us from His Holy Word.

"Therefore, I urge you, brothers, in view of God's mercy, to offer your bodies as living sacrifices, holy and pleasing to God—this is your spiritual[a] act of worship. Do not conform any longer to the pattern of this world, but be transformed by the renewing of your mind. Then you will be able to test and approve what God's will is—his good, pleasing and perfect will" (Rom. 12:1-2).

"Do your best to present yourself to God as one approved, a workman who does not need to be ashamed and who correctly handles the word of truth" (2 Tim. 2:15, NIV).

"Let the word of Christ dwell in you richly as you teach and admonish one another with all wisdom, and as you sing psalms, hymns and spiritual songs with gratitude in your hearts to God" (Col. 3:16, NIV).

"Anyone who receives instruction in the word must share all good things with his instructor" (Gal. 6:6).

We now come to this important moment when you who stand before the altar are to take upon yourselves the task of caring for the affairs of the church and its auxiliary organizations. May you look upon the assignments you now assume as special opportunities for service for our Lord, and may you find joy and spiritual blessing in the performance of your respective duties.

Yours is no light task, for the ongoing of the church and the destiny of souls are in your hands. The development of Christian character is your responsibility, and leading the unsaved to Jesus Christ is your highest objective. May God grant you wisdom and strength as you do His work for His glory.

You have been given a card on which is printed a covenant. We shall read it in unison, and as we do so, let us make it a personal commitment.

Worker's Covenant

Arrange before the service to have a card for each participant with the following printed on it:

In consideration of the confidence placed in me by the church in being selected for the office I now assume, I hereby covenant:

To maintain a high standard of Christian living and example in harmony with the ideals and standards of the Church of the Nazarene.

To cultivate my personal Christian experience by setting aside each day definite time for prayer and Bible reading.

To be present at the regular Sunday School, the Sunday morning and Sunday evening preaching services, and the midweek prayer meeting of the church, unless providentially hindered.

To attend faithfully all duly called meetings of the various boards, councils, or committees to which I have been, or will be, assigned.

To notify my superior officer if I am unable to be present at the stated time, or to carry out my responsibilities in this office.

To read widely the denominational publications and other books and literature that will be helpful to me in discharging the duties of my office.

To improve myself and my skills by participating in Continuing Lay Training courses as opportunity is afforded.

To endeavor to lead people to Jesus Christ by manifesting an active interest in the spiritual welfare of others and by attending and supporting all evangelistic meetings in the church.

The minister shall then offer an appropriate prayer,

and a special song of dedication may be sung, after which the minister shall say:

Having pledged together your hearts and hands to the task of carrying forward the work of this church in your particular assignments, I herewith install you in the respective positions to which you have been elected or appointed. You are now a vital part of the organizational structure and leadership of this church. May you, by example, by precept, and by diligent service, be effective workers in the vineyard of the Lord.

The minister shall ask the congregation to rise and shall address them as follows:

You have heard the pledge and covenant entered into by your church leaders for the coming year. I now charge you, as a congregation, to be loyal in your support of them. The burdens which we have laid upon them are heavy, and they will need your assistance and prayers. May you always be understanding of their problems and tolerant of their seeming failures. May you lend assistance joyfully when called upon, so that, as we work together, our church may be an effective instrument in winning the lost to Christ.

The minister may then lead in a concluding prayer or have the congregation repeat the Lord's Prayer in unison.

Church Dedications

CHURCH DEDICATIONS

Rite One

The dedication of a new church building may be the occasion for a comprehensive dedication of the various components of the facility as well. The dedication of the facilities is most properly understood as the dedication of the people of the church to the proper use of those facilities, which are but the tools through which the church fulfills its mission.

A service of dedication for a new facility may provide occasion for the involvement of many people in the service, thereby broadening the sense of ownership of the objectives and the purposes for which the facility has been constructed or purchased.

The following ritual of dedication presupposes a wide participation of the people of the church and the occasion of dedicating a new facility as well as its furnishings. It is a comprehensive order of service as well as ritual of dedication.

PRELUDE

CALL TO WORSHIP

Pastor: "This is the day the LORD has made; let us rejoice and be glad in it" (Ps. 118:24, NIV).

People: "I was glad when they said unto me, Let us go into the house of the LORD" (Ps. 122:1).

Pastor: "This is none other than the house of God, and this is the gate of heaven" (Gen. 28:17, RSV).

People: The Lord is great beyond all telling; He exceeds all praise. Alleluia, Alleluia.

INVOCATION

The congregation is seated following the invocation.

THE LITURGY OF THE WORD

OLD TESTAMENT LESSON

Two or more readers may be utilized in the following reading.

Reader 1: Then King David rose to his feet and said, . . . "Solomon my son, acknowledge your father's God and serve him with whole heart and willing mind, for the LORD searches all hearts.

Reader 2: "If you search for him, he will let you find him, but if you forsake him, he will cast you off for ever. Remember, then, that the LORD has chosen you to build a house for a sanctuary: be steadfast and do it."

Reader 1: David ordered all the officers of Israel to help Solomon. . . . "Devote yourselves, therefore, heart and soul, to seeking guidance of the LORD your God, and set about building his sanctuary,

Reader 2: "So that the Ark of the Covenant of the LORD and God's holy vessels may be brought into a house built in honour of his name."

Reader 1: Solomon had finished the house of the

Lord. . . . Then Solomon, standing in front of the altar of the LORD, in the presence of the whole assembly . . . , spread out his hands . . . and said,

Reader 2: "O LORD God of Israel, there is no god like thee in heaven or on earth, keeping covenant with thy servants and showing them constant love while they continue faithful to thee in heart and soul. . . . But can God indeed dwell with [mortals] on the earth? Heaven itself, the highest heaven, cannot contain thee; how much less this house that I have built!"

Reader 1: The LORD . . . said, "I have heard your prayer and I have chosen this place. . . . I have chosen and consecrated this house, that my Name may be there for all time and my eyes and my heart be fixed on it."

Unison: Except the LORD build the house, their labor is but lost that build it. This is the LORD's doing; it is marvellous in our eyes *(1 Chron. 28:2, 9-10; 22:17, 19; 2 Chron. 7:11; 6:12, 14, 18; 7:12, 16; see Pss. 127:1; 118:23, all NEB.)*

CONGREGATIONAL SONG: "All Glory, Laud, and Honor"

NEW TESTAMENT LESSON

Reader 1: But now in Christ Jesus you who once were far off have been brought near by the blood of

Christ. . . . So then you are no longer strangers, but . . . members of the household of God, built upon the foundation of the apostles and prophets, with Christ Jesus himself as the [chief] cornerstone.

Reader 2: In him the whole structure is joined together and grows into a holy temple in the Lord. . . . In him you too are being built with all the rest into a spiritual dwelling for God.

Reader 1: Therefore come to him, a living stone, though rejected by mortals yet chosen and precious in God's sight, and like living stones, let yourselves be built into a spiritual house, . . . acceptable to God through Jesus Christ. For it stands in scripture:

"See, I am laying in Zion a stone,
a cornerstone chosen and precious;
and whoever believes in him
will not be put to shame."

Reader 2: "The stone that the builders rejected has become the very head of the corner." . . . The household of God is the church of the living God, the pillar and bulwark of the truth.

Unison: There can be no other foundation beyond that which is already laid; I mean Jesus Christ himself *(Eph. 2:13, 19-21, NRSV; v. 22, NEB; 1 Pet. 2:4-7; 1 Tim. 3:15, all NRSV; 1 Cor. 3:11, NEB).*

WELCOME AND INTRODUCTIONS

PRESENTATION OF THE SANCTUARY

Here the symbolic presentation of the keys to the building to the pastor by the chairperson of the Building Committee may be made. If the contractor is present, he or she may be asked to participate in the presentation as well.

DEDICATION OF THE SANCTUARY BUILDING
FOR THE WORSHIP OF THE HOLY TRINITY

Pastor: Beloved in the Lord, we rejoice that God has put it into the hearts of His people to build this house to the glory of His name. Let us now dedicate it to the worship of our God, Father, Son, and Holy Spirit, and to the service of all persons for whom Christ died.

To the worship of God the Father, who created us and loves us.

People: We dedicate this house.

Pastor: To the glory of God the Son, who redeemed us by His grace.

People: We dedicate this house.

Pastor: To the honor of the Holy Spirit, who sanctifies and guides us.

People: We dedicate this house.

DEDICATORY RESPONSE

Here the district superintendent or pastor may briefly

respond to the dedication of the building with appropriate remarks.

DEDICATORY PRAYERS

PRAYER TO GOD THE FATHER

A member of the church board may be asked to read this prayer, expressed on behalf of the people.

Ever living Father, watchful and caring, our Creator and our End: All that we have and all that we are is Yours. Accept us now as we dedicate this place to which we come to praise Your name, to ask Your forgiveness, to know Your healing power, to hear Your Word, and to be nourished by the body and blood of Your Son. Be present always to guide and to judge, to illumine, and to bless Your people.

PRAYER TO GOD THE SON

A member of the congregation may be asked to read this prayer on behalf of the people.

Lord Jesus Christ, our Redeemer, make this a temple of Your presence and a house of prayer. Be always near us when we seek You in this place. Draw us to You, when we come alone and when we come with others, to find comfort and wisdom, to be supported and strengthened, to rejoice and give thanks. May it be here, Lord Christ, that we are made one with You and with one another, so that our lives are sustained and sanctified to Your service.

PRAYER TO GOD THE HOLY SPIRIT

A member of the congregation, perhaps a young person, could be asked to read this prayer on behalf of the congregation.

God, Holy Spirit, Sanctifier of the faithful, open our eyes, our ears, and our hearts that we may grow closer to You through joy and through suffering. Be with us in the fullness of Your power as new members are added to Your household, as we grow in grace through the years, when we are joined in marriage, when we turn to You in sickness or special need, and, at last, when we are committed into the Father's hands. O Father, Son, and Holy Spirit, whom we worship as one God, sanctify this place.

CONGREGATIONAL SONG: "Holy, Holy, Holy"

DEDICATION OF THE PULPIT

LITANY OF DEDICATION

A member of the church board or the pastor may be asked to lead this portion of the litany.

Reader: Grant, O Lord, that Your holy Word will be faithfully read and preached from this sacred desk.

People: Your Word is a lamp to guide our feet.

Reader: Grant, O Lord, that the hearers of the gospel proclaimed here will understand what You are calling them to do and will receive the strength to answer the divine call.

People: Your Word is a light upon our path.

Reader: Grant, O Lord, that sinners will find salvation and believers will find the highway of holiness through the preaching that comes from this pulpit.

People: Your prophetic Word is a light that shines in a dark place, until the day dawns and the morning star rises in our hearts.

Reader: Grant, O Lord, that as the hungry and those wandering in darkness sit before this pulpit, they shall be fed the Bread of Life, and they shall see the Light of the World.

People: The unfolding of Your Word gives light and wisdom even to the simple and unlearned.

Reader: We dedicate this pulpit in the name of the Father, Son, and Holy Spirit.

People: Amen and alleluia.

DEDICATION OF THE ALTAR

A SEVENFOLD PRAYER OF DEDICATION

A member of the church or staff involved in evangelism may be asked to lead this portion of the litany.

Reader: O God, we now dedicate this altar as a place of prayer. From this day forward let those who would offer prayers of repentance for sin kneel here.

People: O God, when Your people sin against You but then return to You with all their heart and soul, hear from heaven and forgive them.

Reader: Let those who would offer prayers of confession, of need, kneel here.

People: Our sins are higher than our head, our guilt has reached to the heavens.

Reader: Let those who would consecrate their lives to God kneel here.

People: By the mercies of God we present our bodies as a living sacrifice.

Reader: Let those in need of saving or sanctifying grace kneel here.

People: May the God of peace himself sanctify us through and through.

Reader: Let those who need courage, strength, and wisdom kneel here.

People: The fear of the Lord is the beginning of wisdom.

Reader: Let those who sorrow with groanings too deep for words kneel here.

People: The Spirit himself makes intercession for us with groanings which cannot be uttered.

Reader: Let those who before this altar are joined in holy matrimony kneel here.

People: What God has joined together let not mortals put asunder.

DEDICATION OF THE BAPTISTERY

PRAYER OF DEDICATION

The pastor or other congregational leader may read the prayer.

Grant, O Lord, that this baptistery, which we now hallow for Thy service, may powerfully symbolize the "washing of regeneration" to all those who shall be baptized therein. May they be truly washed and purified by the Holy Spirit. May they truly die unto sin and rise again unto righteousness, and always remain in the assembly of Your faithful children, through Jesus Christ our Lord.

People: There is one Lord, one faith, one baptism, one God and Father of all, to whom we dedicate this baptistery. Amen and alleluia.

DEDICATION OF THE TABLE OF THE LORD

The pastor may lead this portion of the litany.

The table of the Lord is, first of all, a symbol of redemption. Here we focus our worship upon the shed blood and broken body of our Lord, Jesus Christ. Each time we gaze upon it we are reminded that we are redeemed by His blood, saved by His grace.

We now hallow this table for the celebration of the sacrament of Jesus' broken body and shed blood. Whenever we see it, kneel before it, partake of its bread and wine, we will be reminded that He died for us, redeemed us by His blood, sustains us on our journey, and that He, the Bread of Life, is coming again.

People: This is the Bread which comes down from heaven; that one may eat thereof and not die.

CONGREGATIONAL SONG: "When I Survey the Wondrous Cross"

PRAYER OF DEDICATION

The pastor may read this prayer.

Grant, O God, that whosoever shall receive at this table the blessed sacrament of the blood and body of Thy Son may receive all the benefits of His poured out love and grace. Give to the communicants a penitent heart, forgiveness for transgression, a fervent hope in Christ, confirmation of salvation, strength to carry out God's will, loyalty to the Church of Jesus Christ, an abiding love for others, and a treasured expectation for the coming again of our Lord. Through Jesus Christ our Lord. Amen.

CONSECRATION OF THE MUSIC FOR WORSHIP

The leader of music may lead this portion of the litany. The responses are taken from selected portions of 2 Chron. 5:11-14 and Ps. 126, usu. NRSV.

Leader: The priests came out of the holy place, and all the levitical singers, their children and kindred with them, arrayed in fine linen, with cymbals, harps, and lyres.

People: Then our mouth was filled with laughter, and our tongue with shouts of joy.

Leader: The trumpeters and singers made themselves heard in unison in praise and thanksgiving to the LORD.

People: The LORD has done great things for us, and we rejoiced.

Leader: And when they raised with one voice the song:
"For he is good,
for his steadfast love endures forever,"
then the house, the house of the LORD,
was filled with a cloud; for the glory,
the glory of the LORD filled the house.

People: Those who sow in tears
shall reap in joy.
Those who go out weeping,
bearing precious seed,
shall come home with shouts of joy,
bringing with them their sheaves.

DEDICATORY RESPONSE

Here the director of music may briefly make appropriate remarks in receiving the facilities and furnishings for the music of worship.

PRAYER OF DEDICATION

The pastor may read this prayer.

O God, Your people worship You with many voices and sounds, in times of joy and sorrow. Move us to express the wonder, the power, and the glory of Your creation and redemption in the music we make and in the songs we sing.

People: Praise God in His sanctuary.
Praise Him with the sound of the trumpet.
Praise Him with strings and pipe.
Praise Him according to His excellent greatness.
Amen and alleluia.

CHOIR

Suitable hymns or anthems would include "Christ Is Made the Sure Foundation" or "The Church's One Foundation." Following the music, the music leader and the congregation may be invited to read responsively as follows:

Leader: What a foundation we stand on now: the apostles and the prophets; and the cornerstone of the building is Jesus Christ himself! We who believe are carefully joined together with Christ as parts of a beautiful, constantly growing temple for God *(Eph. 2:20-21, TLB)*.

People:
The Church's one foundation
    Is Jesus Christ, her Lord.
She is His new creation
    By water and the Word.
From heaven He came and sought her
    To be His holy bride;
With His own blood He bought her,
    And for her life He died.

Yet she on earth hath union
    With God, the Three in One,
And mystic, sweet communion
    With those whose rest is won.
O happy ones and holy!
    Lord, give us grace that we,
Like them, the meek and lowly,
    On high may dwell with Thee.

—Samuel J. Stone

THE DEDICATORY SERMON

THE DEDICATION OF THE PEOPLE OF GOD

The pastor or other congregational leader may read the following.

You are God's building. Surely you know that you are God's temple, where the Spirit of God dwells. . . . The temple of God is holy; and that temple you are.

Do you not know that your bodies are limbs and organs of Christ? Do you not know that your body is a shrine of the indwelling Holy Spirit, and the Spirit is God's gift to you? . . . You are not your own; you were bought with a price.

The temple of the living God is what we are. God's own words are:

"I will live and move about among them;

I will be their God, and they shall be my people."

And therefore, ". . . Touch nothing unclean. . . .

I will be a father to you,

and you shall be my sons and daughters."

Therefore, . . . let us cleanse ourselves from all filthiness of the flesh and spirit, perfecting holiness in the fear of God *(1 Cor. 3:9, 16-17; 6:15, 19, all NEB; vv. 19-20, RSV; 2 Cor. 6:16-18, NEB; 7:1)*.

PROCLAMATION OF DEDICATION

Pastor: We have dedicated this building and its contents. Yet we know that the true church is not made of brick and stone but people. Whatever else the church may be called, it is, according to the Scripture, a called-out community of faith.

God dwells with and within His people. They form His temple "not made with hands." His very seat of dwelling is in their hearts. The Bible uses the term *naos*. That is a word used by the ancient Greeks to refer to the very niche in a pagan temple where the idol or image of the temple god or goddess was placed. Paul tells us that our hearts, by God's grace, have become the very niche where the true God dwells.

This behooves us to purify God's *naos,* His niche within, to cleanse and rededicate our whole being to His service.

Will you dedicate, again this day, your heart and your life to the service of God, both in this sanctuary and the great chapel of God that is the world?

Congregation: We will and do so dedicate ourselves.

PRAYER FOR THE DEDICATION OF THE PEOPLE OF GOD

Here the district superintendent, or the pastor, may lead the litany.

Let us signify our dedication to God as a called-out community of faith by praying together.

Congregation:
Almighty God, to whom all hearts are open,
all desires known,
and from whom no secrets are hidden,
cleanse the thoughts of our hearts,
by the inspiration of Your Holy Spirit,
so that we may perfectly love You,
and worthily magnify Your holy name.
Through Jesus Christ our Lord. Amen.[13]

CONGREGATIONAL SONG: "For Such a Time as This"

CLOSING PRAYER

POSTLUDE

Rite Two

The following ritual is a more abbreviated rite of dedication, found in the *Manual of the Church of the Nazarene.*

Minister: Having been prospered by the hand of the Lord and enabled by His grace and strength to complete this building to the glory of His name, we now stand in God's presence to dedicate this structure to the service of His kingdom.

To the glory of God our Father, from whom cometh every good and perfect gift; to the honor of Jesus Christ, our Lord and Savior; and to the praise of the Holy Spirit, Source of light, and life, and power—our Sanctifier,

Congregation: We do now, with joy and gratitude, humbly dedicate this building.

Minister: In remembrance of all who have loved and served this church, establishing the heritage we now enjoy, and who are now part of the Church Triumphant,

Congregation: We gratefully dedicate this edifice (sanctuary, education building, fellowship hall, etc.).

Minister: For worship in prayer and song, for the preaching of the Word, for the teaching of the Scriptures, and for the fellowship of the saints,

Congregation: We solemnly dedicate this house of God.

Minister: For the comfort of those who mourn, for the strengthening of the weak, for the help of those who are tempted, and for the giving of hope and courage to all who come within these walls,

Congregation: We dedicate this place of fellowship and prayer.

Minister: For the sharing of the good news of salvation from sin, for the spreading of scriptural holiness, for the giving of instruction in righteousness, and for the service of our fellowmen,

Congregation: We reverently dedicate this building.

Unison: We, as laborers together with God, now join hands and hearts and dedicate ourselves anew to the high and holy purposes to which this building has been set apart. We pledge our loyal devotion, faithful stewardship, and diligent service to the end that in this place the name of the Lord shall be glorified, and His kingdom shall be advanced; through Jesus Christ our Lord. Amen.

LITANY FOR CLOSING A SANCTUARY[14]

This litany is intended for use when a new sanctuary is being prepared and the congregation wishes to give acknowledgment and gratitude for the previous place of worship that has served their needs and been the site from which they have moved in service to Christ and the world around.

Minister: Let us give thanks to Almighty God for mercies bestowed here in past years.

For the erection and dedication of this house to Your honor and glory as a place of worship, preaching, and service, and for the witness in faith and life that has here been given to the people of these generations,

People: We thank You, Lord.

Minister: For all those servants of God who have led Your people in worship here, who have preached Your Word from this pulpit, and who have administered the sacraments to waiting and believing hearts,

People: We thank You, Lord.

Minister: For sacred song and music, for drama and story and ceremony that have helped people see the objectives and directions of Christian living,

People: We thank You, Lord.

Minister: For all those who have come to this place seeking You, and who, in worshiping You in spirit and in truth, have found You,

People: We thank You, Lord.

Minister: For those who have brought their children here for Christian baptism or dedication, for those who have pledged their love to one another at Your holy altar, and for those who in Christian faith and trust have here parted with a loved one and committed that loved one to Your love and care,

People: We thank You, Lord.

Minister: For sins that have been confessed and forgiven here, for burdens that have been made easier to carry, for distressed and troubled hearts that have known the peace that passes all understanding, and for lives that have been inspired to new heights of love and service, for hearts that have been cleansed, and lives that have been possessed of the love of God and humankind,

People: We thank You, Lord.

Minister: For all this building has meant to congregation, visitor, and town; for the walls of security, the overarching of love, the support of encouragement, the halls of friendship, the lessons of humanity, the lights of faith, and the doorways to service,

People: We thank You, Lord.

Minister: Bless us, we pray, as we go from here; and, as our new church home grows about us, may we be bound together in the glorious adventure of building for You a house of life and heart and service, to the glory of Your name and the extending of Your kingdom, in the name of the Creator and of the Son and of the Holy Spirit.

Unison: Now unto Him who is able to keep us from falling, and to present us faultless before the presence of His glory with exceeding joy, to the only wise God, our Savior, be glory and majesty, dominion and power, both now and forever.

Minister: The grace of our Lord Jesus Christ, the love of God, and the communion of the Holy Spirit be with you evermore. Amen.

The minister hands the pulpit Bible to the secretary of the congregation, and the official board escorts it from the sanctuary. The Bible represents the people's place of worship, and this action shows that the place of worship will be in the care of the official board until the dedication of a new building, at which time it will be placed on the pulpit of the new church home.

RITUAL FOR THE DEDICATION OF A PARSONAGE[15]

Minister: In the name of God, the Creator, and of the Son and of the Holy Spirit. Amen.

People: We have assembled here to dedicate this house unto God.

Trustee: As those to whom the responsibility of maintaining this house has been committed, we now express our willingness to dedicate it unto Him who is the Master Builder and the Keeper of all, whose we are and whom we serve.

Minister: To what ends and for what purposes do you wish to dedicate this house?

Unison: As a fitting and pleasant place where our pastor and family can make their home.

As a place where study and meditation on the Holy Scripture may be pursued.

As a place where Christian fellowship may be had, where we have shared both our joys and our sorrows, our successes and our shortcomings, and strengthen the ties that bind our hearts in Christian love.

As a place where the confidential counsel of God's ministering servant can be found.

And as a quiet and comfortable place of refuge and relief to which God's servant can return when at times the duties and responsibilities of the office bear heavily.

To these ends and for the glory of God, we now dedicate this parsonage.

Minister: O God, You have heard the expressed desires of these Your people for whose spiritual well-being I am responsible. Accept, we ask You, this house that they with their gifts and their labor do provide and shall endeavor to maintain.

Grant indeed, gracious God, that we may all do our part to keep it always for the high purposes to which they have now pledged it. And may all who shall ever dwell herein live lives that bear steadfast witness to the Savior, that Your blessed and holy benediction may rest upon it now and as long as it shall stand.

In the name of Jesus Christ, our Lord. Amen.

Unison:

Bless this house, O Lord, we pray,
Make it safe by night and day;
Bless these walls, so firm and stout,
Keeping want and trouble out;
Bless the roof and chimneys tall,
Let Thy peace lie over all;
Bless this door, that it may prove
Ever open to joy and love.
Bless these windows shining bright,

Letting in God's heavenly light;
Bless the hearth ablazing there,
With smoke ascending like a prayer;
Bless the folk who dwell within,
Keep them pure and free from sin;
Bless us all that we may be
Fit, O Lord, to dwell with Thee,
Bless us all that one day we
May dwell, O Lord, with Thee. Amen.‡

—Helen Taylor

RITUAL FOR THE DEDICATION OF A HOME‡

DEDICATION OF A HOME

Minister: Peace be to this house,

People: And to all who dwell therein.

Minister: Our help is in the name of the Lord,

People: Who made heaven and earth.

Minister: Peace be within your walls,

People: And prosperity within your palaces.

Minister: For my brothers', sisters', and friends' sakes, I will now say:

People: Peace be with you. Glory be to the Father and to the Son and to the Holy Ghost. As it was in the beginning, is now, and ever shall be, world without end. Amen.

SCRIPTURE: *Prov. 24:3-4*

Minister: Let us pray. O Lord God, Your gifts are many, and in wisdom You have made all things to give You glory. We ask You to bless those who live in this place. Visit with Your love and gladness all who come and go, and preserve us all in peace, through Jesus Christ our Lord. Amen.

‡Reprinted from *Occasional Services*, copyright © 1982, used by permission of Augsburg Fortress.

A CANDLE IS LIGHTED

SCRIPTURE: *Matt. 5:14-16*

Minister: Let us pray. O God, as this candle gives light to this home, so enable those who dwell here to be Your light in the world, through Jesus Christ our Lord. Amen.

SCRIPTURE: *Matt. 7:24-27*

Minister: Let us pray. O God, from whom the whole family in heaven and earth is named, be present in this home, that all who live here, having genuine affection for one another, may find here a haven of blessing and of peace, through Jesus Christ our Lord. Amen.

SCRIPTURE: *Luke 19:1-10*

Minister: Let us pray. O God, refresh all who visit here, that they may know friendship and love, through Jesus Christ our Lord. Amen.

SCRIPTURE: *Ps. 121:8*

Minister: Let us pray. O God, protect and guide those who live here, their going out and their coming in; and let them share the hospitality of this home with all who visit, that those who enter here may know Your love and peace, through Jesus Christ our Lord. Amen.

SCRIPTURE: *John 13:34-35*

Minister: Let us pray. O God, be present with those who come here for fellowship and recreation, that they may be renewed and refreshed, through Jesus Christ our Lord. Amen.

SCRIPTURE: *Acts 2:46-47*

Minister: Let us pray. To live with You, O Lord, is to be at home with ourselves. Now be with us, we pray, as we dedicate this place as a home for _____ _____. Bless these personal things of taste and choice that put the mark of these particular people upon it and make it theirs. May it be a place of shelter and protection, of rest and healing, of warmth and hospitality. And may Your embracing love be seen and felt in all the celebrations, daily chores, hard decisions, and shared glories that will occur here. As it will become the storehouse of blessed memories, make it also a place for growth in grace. We pray in the name of Him who has prepared a place for us, in whose house are many rooms, even Jesus Christ our Lord. Amen.

LORD'S PRAYER

Minister: The Lord watch over our going out and our coming in from this time forth forever. Amen.

DOXOLOGY

Other Rituals

SEASONAL SERVICES

Advent

The following services are designed to guide a church in the celebration of Advent, which is the beginning of the Christian year. The season of Advent begins with the fourth Sunday before Christmas, which is the Sunday nearest November 30, and continues to Christmas Eve. The word "Advent" derives from the Latin *adventus,* which means "coming." The season proclaims the comings of Christ—whose birth we prepare to celebrate once again, who comes continually in Word and Spirit, and whose return in final victory we anticipate. Therefore, Advent looks both backward to Jesus' first coming at Bethlehem and forward to His coming again at the end.

We begin the Christian year by reflecting on the end of history. The message of many of the Advent hymns have a note of threat and promise in contrast to the more traditional Christmas carols. This emphasis points to the thrust of the readings and sermons most usually associated with Advent. Those churches that utilize the Revised Common Lectionary, or other ordered readings in conjunction with the observance of the Christian year, find that the readings for Advent deal not so much with preparation for Christmas as with the expectation of Christ's return in glory to rule, judge, and save. The prayer of this season is expressed in the phrases of the Lord's Prayer: "Thy kingdom come, thy will be done, on earth" (Matt. 6:10, RSV). There is a strong prophetic note in this season announcing judgment upon evil, combined with an emphasis on hope and the expectation of Christ's coming reign in glory.

159

Various colors and combinations of colors are suggested for use during Advent and Christmas. Purple or blue banners and paramounts are suggested for Advent, while white, yellow, and gold are suggested for the celebration of Christmas Eve and Day.

The Advent wreath, often used in churches and in homes, is an evergreen wreath with four purple candles and a central white Christ candle added or lighted on Christmas Eve or Christmas Day.

The Hanging of the Greens[16]

Some churches celebrate the beginning of Advent with a service of the Hanging of the Greens. Other churches observe the service at other times during Advent. The service may be used on a Sunday morning during the opening of the service or as a response to the Word. It may also be used as an evening service. During the singing of "Come, Thou Long-expected Jesus," greens may be brought in and the Advent candle lighted.

In the service of the Hanging of the Greens, each of the lessons should, if possible, be read by a different reader. Each reader should announce the lesson by the descriptive title preceding it. At the end of the lesson, the reader or another person reads the narrative.

INTRODUCTION*

Reader 1: How shall we prepare this house for the coming of the King?

Reader 2: With branches of cedar, the tree of royalty.

Reader 1: How shall we prepare this house for the coming of the eternal Christ?

Reader 2: With garlands of pine and fir, whose leaves are ever living, ever green.

Reader 1: How shall we prepare this house for the coming of our Savior?

Reader 2: With wreaths of holly and ivy, telling of His passion, death, and resurrection.

Reader 1: How shall we prepare our hearts for the coming of the Son of God?

Reader 2: By hearing again the words of the prophets, who foretold the saving work of God.

Reader 1: For God did not send the Son into the world to condemn the world, but that the world through him might be saved.

Reader 2: Glory to God in the highest!

GOD WILL SEND A RIGHTEOUS KING (Jer. 23:5-6)

Reader 3: In ancient times the cedar was revered as the tree of royalty.

It also signified immortality and was used for purification.

We place this cedar branch as a sign of Christ, who reigns as King forever, and whose coming, in justice and righteousness, will purify our hearts.

HYMN

Suggested hymns: "Come, Thou Long-expected Jesus," *Sing to the Lord* (STTL), 157; "Jesus Shall Reign," STTL, 271; "Rejoice, the Lord Is King," STTL, 276

THE PROPHET DECLARES A CHILD WILL BE BORN (Isa. 9:2, 6-7)

Because the needles of pine and fir trees appear not to

die each season, the ancients saw them as signs of things that last forever. Isaiah tells us that there will be no end to the reign of the Messiah. Therefore, we hang this wreath of evergreens shaped in a circle, which itself has no end, to signify the eternal reign of Jesus, the Christ.

HYMN

> Suggested hymn: "O Come, O Come, Emmanuel," STTL, 163

THE FOURTH SERVANT SONG (Isa. 53:1-6)

For Christians, this passage from Isaiah reflects the sufferings of Jesus, who saved us from our sins by His death on the Cross and by His resurrection from the dead.

In ancient times, holly and ivy were considered signs of Christ's passion. Their prickly leaves suggested the crown of thorns, the red berries the blood of the Savior, and the bitter bark the drink offered to Jesus on the Cross.

As we hang the holly and the ivy, let us rejoice in the coming of Jesus, our Savior.

HYMN

> Suggested hymns: "I Lay My Sins on Jesus," STTL, 340; "I Know a Fount," STTL, 252

THE MYSTERY OF THE INCARNATION*
(John 1:1-5, 9-14)

As we prepare for the coming of Jesus, the Light of the World, we light the Christmas tree. During this Advent, wherever you see a lighted Christmas tree, let it call to mind the One who brings light to our darkness, healing to our brokenness, and peace to all who receive Him.

The tree is now lighted.

HYMN

Suggested hymn: "Emmanuel," STTL, 165

THE BLESSING OF THE TREE

Many churches allow children to participate in bringing decorations for the tree. In some cases, use of a Christmas tree encourages those who decorate the tree to use symbolic decorations that depict some dimension of the life and ministry of Christ, such as stars, fish, or other symbols. A blessing is pronounced for the tree and its meaning, often preceded by the reading of Titus 3:4-7. In some churches, the tree trunk is saved to make a cross for Lent. The following blessing is suggested for use:

Holy Lord,

we come with joy to celebrate the birth of your Son,
who rescued us from the darkness of sin
by making the cross a tree of life and light.

May this tree, arrayed in splendor,
remind us of the life-giving cross of Christ,

that we may always rejoice
in the new life that shines on our hearts.

We ask this through Christ our Lord.

Amen.[17]

BLESSINGS OF THE ADVENT WREATH

> The Advent wreath is a simple circle of evergreen branches, a sign of life without end; its four Advent candles encircle a central white Christ candle. Some traditions use the color rose on the third Sunday of Advent and for this reason use three purple candles and one rose candle. The following blessing, with a reading from Isa. 9:2, 6-7, may precede the lighting of the first Advent candle. This blessing may also be used for blessing an Advent wreath in a home.

Reader 1: Christ came to bring us salvation and has promised to come again.

Let us pray that we may always be ready to welcome Him.

Reader 2: Come, Lord Jesus.

Reader 1: Let us pray that the keeping of Advent may open our hearts to God's love.

Reader 2: Come, Lord Jesus.

Reader 1: Let us pray that the light of Christ may penetrate the darkness of sin.

Reader 2: Come, Lord Jesus.

Reader 1: Let us pray that this wreath may constantly remind us to prepare for the coming of Christ.

Reader 2: Come, Lord Jesus.

Reader 1: Let us pray that the Christmas season may fill us with peace and joy as we strive to follow the example of Jesus.

Reader 2: Come, Lord Jesus.

Reader 1: Loving God, Your Church joyfully awaits the coming of its Savior, who enlightens our hearts and dispels the darkness of ignorance and sin.

Pour forth Your blessings upon us as we light the candles of this wreath.

May their light reflect the splendor of Christ, who is Lord, for ever and ever. Amen.[18]

LIGHTING OF THE ADVENT CANDLES

Each Sunday of Advent may include the lighting of the Advent candles by an appointed family or person. This is usually done early in the service. Each Sunday one additional candle is lighted until all four are lighted. Finally, on Christmas Eve and Day, the middle white candle is lighted. The person lighting the candles, or another assisting them, may say the words provided for each Sunday. The candles may be lighted during or after the reading of the Scripture lessons or while a hymn is sung or other appropriate words are spoken.

Suggested Readings:

First Sunday—Isa. 60:2-3

We light this candle as a symbol of Christ our Hope.

May the light sent from God shine in the darkness to show us the way of salvation.

O come, O come, Emmanuel.

Second Sunday—Mark 1:4

We light this candle as a symbol of Christ the Way.

May the Word sent from God through the prophets lead us to the way of salvation.

O come, O come, Emmanuel.

Third Sunday—Isa. 35:10

We light this candle as a symbol of Christ our Joy.

May the joyful promise of Your presence, O God, make us rejoice in our hope of salvation.

O come, O come, Emmanuel.

Fourth Sunday—Isa. 9:6-7

We light this candle as a symbol of the Prince of Peace.

May the visitation of Your Holy Spirit, O God, make us ready for the coming of Jesus, our Hope and Joy.

O come, O come, Emmanuel.[19]

Creative Worship Bulletin Ideas
for Christmas[20]

First Sunday of Advent

There's a Song in the Air
We are greeted in the name of the Lord Jesus.
The pastor shares.
We prepare our hearts for worship.

There's a Star in the Sky
The choir calls us to worship.
The lighting of the Advent wreath.
†Congregational hymn.
Congregational hymn.*

There's a Tumult of Joy
A moment for friendship.
We worship with His tithes and our offerings.
Congregational hymn.
We come into His presence.
Bring your needs to the altar.
Scripture reading.

We Rejoice in the Light
The sanctuary choir.
Silent prayer for our pastor.
Today's good news by the pastor.

Second Sunday of Advent

Come, Thou Long-expected Jesus
God's forever family gathers.
Share a moment with the pastor.
Quietly ask God's blessing upon the service.
Meditate upon Luke 2.

Born to Set Thy People Free
The choir calls us to worship.
We celebrate Advent as we sing a hymn.*
The lighting of the Advent wreath.
Congregational hymn.

Israel's Strength and Consolation
It is family altar time.
The choir calls us to prayer.
We bring our praise and petitions to the altar.
The choir ministers to us.
A moment for friendship.
We worship with His tithes and our offerings.
Special music.

Joy of Every Longing Heart
Today's good news by the pastor.
Closing hymn.*

Third Sunday of Advent

Hark! the Herald Angels Sing
The pastor greets us.
We prepare our hearts for worship.

Glory to the Newborn King!
The choir calls us to worship.
The lighting of the Advent wreath.
†Congregational hymn.
Congregational hymn.*

Veiled in Flesh the Godhead See
A moment for friendship.
We worship with His tithes and our offerings.
Congregational hymn.
We come into His presence.
Bring your needs to the altar.
Scripture reading.

Hail th'incarnate Deity!
The sanctuary choir.
Silent prayer for our pastor.
Today's good news by the pastor.

Fourth Sunday of Advent

O Come, All Ye Faithful
A Christmas greeting.
A moment for reflection.

Yea, Lord, We Greet Thee
The choir leads us in praise and adoration.
We share in the Christmas event by singing a hymn.*
The lighting of the Advent wreath.

Come and Behold Him
The choir calls us to prayer.
The Christmas altar is open.
We bring to King Jesus our gifts.
We ask for help with our needs.
Sanctuary choir.
We present to our Lord His tithes and our offerings.
A moment for friendship.

Word of the Father
Special music.
Today's good news by the pastor.
Closing hymn.*

A Service of Carols and Candles

ORGAN PRELUDE

THE PROCESSIONAL CHRISTMAS CAROL

The congregation will rise as the choir enters.

"O Come, All Ye Faithful" (Adeste Fidelis, trans. Frederick Oakeley et al.)

THE CALL TO WORSHIP

Minister: "In the beginning was the Word."

People: "And the Word was with God, and the Word was God."

Minister: "All things were made by him."

People: "And without him was not any thing made that was made."

Minister: "In him was life."

People: "And the life was the light of men."

Unison: Let our light so shine before men, that they may see our good works, and glorify our Father in heaven. Amen!

The congregation will be seated.

The Light Revealed

A PROPHECY
Isa. 9:6-7; Luke 1:26-33

A CHRISTMAS CAROL

> Congregation and choir

> "O Little Town of Bethlehem" (Phillips Brooks)

The Light Received

A CHRISTMAS SCRIPTURE READING—LUKE 2:1-18

A CHRISTMAS CAROL

> Congregation and choir

> "It Came upon the Midnight Clear" (Edmund H. Sears)

THE CHRISTMAS OFFERING

A CHRISTMAS ANTHEM

> The choir

THE CHRISTMAS PRAYER

A CHRISTMAS MEDITATION

A CHRISTMAS CAROL

> Congregation and choir

> "Hark! the Herald Angels Sing" (Charles Wesley)

The Light Reflected
(A Service of Lights)

THE DISTRIBUTION OF CANDLES

> The pastor will light his candle; the ushers will light their candles from the pastor's candle; the ushers will

then move down the aisle, lighting the candles of the congregation in this manner: The worshipers nearest the center aisle will receive the light and in turn give their light to the one by their side. "Silent Night!" should be sung softly and reverently, with no other light burning but the candles. The candles should not be extinguished until the close of the Lord's Prayer.

A CHRISTMAS CAROL

Congregation standing

"Silent Night!" (Joseph Mohr, trans. John F. Young)

THE CLOSING PRAYER OF DEDICATION

Followed by the Lord's Prayer

BENEDICTION

THE RECESSIONAL CHRISTMAS CAROL

Congregation and choir

"Joy to the World" (Isaac Watts, Antioch)

ORGAN POSTLUDE

Christmas Sunday

Welcome and Merry Christmas! It is Christmas Sunday, and what joy it is to celebrate the birth of our Lord and Savior Jesus Christ, in His house, with His people. Today we celebrate not only His original coming but His coming into our hearts individually and the promise of His return to unite us with Him forever. Our joining with the sights and sounds of the Advent season is now complete. Come, let us worship our King!

ORGAN PRELUDE

WE ARE CALLED TO CELEBRATE

Through music: "He Is Born"

Sanctuary choir and balcony brass

Through the reading of Scripture: Luke 2:21-35
Through our Advent liturgy

See below

WE CELEBRATE IN SONG

"Joy to the World" (Isaac Watts)

"I Heard the Bells on Christmas Day" (Henry W. Longfellow)

"O Come, All Ye Faithful" (trans. Frederick Oakeley et al.)

WE JOIN OUR HEARTS AND MINDS IN PRAYER

Refrain: "O Come, Let Us Adore Him"
Pastoral prayer

"Simeon took him in his arms and praised God" (Luke 2:28, NIV). We would do as Simeon did.

OUR WORSHIP CELEBRATION CONTINUES

Through music: "Simeon's Song"

Sanctuary choir and balcony brass

As we fellowship
As we give

Offertory

We Are Ministered to

In song: "Let This Child Be Born in You"

Sanctuary choir and balcony brass

By message from the Word: "Simeon Saw Salvation in a Baby"

We Respond

Our Prayer of Benediction

We depart "praising God, and saying, Glory to God in the highest, and on earth peace, good will toward men" (Luke 2:13-14).

Come Share the Joy!

Advent Candle Liturgy

First Reader: Today is the fourth and last Sunday of Advent. We return again to the festive wreath with the question, "What do you see?"

Second Reader: The first candle represents Zechariah, who saw an angel but also saw reconciliation between God and man.

First Reader: The second candle stands for the magi, who saw a star and recognized sovereignty.

Second Reader: The third candle stands for the shepherds, who saw a Savior in a manger.

First Reader: This fourth candle represents Simeon, whose eyes longed to see "the consolation of Israel."

176

Second Reader: He saw a baby in His mother's arms. But he saw more. He saw "the Lord's Christ"! And he rejoiced.

First Reader: We also see the Lord's Christ in Jesus.

Second Reader: And we rejoice!

Easter[21]

Tenebrae Service

The Vigil of Darkness
A Service of Lights

PRELUDE

"There Is a Fountain"

Handbell choir

INTRODUCTION TO THE TENEBRAE SERVICE

INVOCATION

Minister: Let us pray. O God, this is a night filled with memory and hope. Let us remember.

People: And so we remember that we are made of clay, molded in Your image.

Minister: We think about yesterday and sigh; and we are anxious about tomorrow.

People: May Your presence fill the room and remove the guilt of yesterday and give us purpose for tomorrow. Remind us again that we are accepted.

Minister: Make our acceptance of ourselves and each other complete through Christ our Lord. Amen.

FIRST LIGHT

The Darkness of Betrayal
Hymn: "O Jesus, I Have Promised"

SECOND LIGHT

The Darkness of Desertion
Hymn: "O Love That Will Not Let Me Go"

THIRD LIGHT

The Darkness of Disunity
Hymn: "'Tis Midnight"

FOURTH LIGHT

The Darkness of Disloyalty
Hymn: "Must Jesus Bear the Cross Alone?"

FIFTH LIGHT

The Darkness of Denial
Chancel choir: "Beneath the Cross of Jesus"

SIXTH LIGHT

The Darkness of the Cross
Chancel choir: "O Sacred Head, Now Wounded"

THE SACRAMENT OF HOLY COMMUNION

TRIO

"Precious Blood"

SEVENTH LIGHT

The Darkness of Light
Hymn: "On the Cross of Calvary"

BENEDICTION

Minister: "For, behold, the darkness shall cover the earth, and gross darkness the people."

People: "But the LORD shall arise upon thee, and his glory shall be seen upon thee."

Minister: "And the Gentiles shall come to thy light, and kings to the brightness of thy rising."

People: Lord, Thou hast broken bread with us in fellowship, and Thy broken body reminds us of our death. Break this fellowship and scatter us out upon Thy world, and by Thy grace bring us together again at Thy table, through Him who is the Light of the World, even Jesus Christ, our Lord. Amen.

POSTLUDE

—Courtesy of Robert Simmons

Tenebrae Service
by Virginia Cameron

Two varied examples of a Tenebrae service outline are provided here for your referral. Note that instructions and a brief explanation as to the history and nature of the service are included in the bulletin or worship folder for each worshiper.

The beauty of this service is its simplicity and its adaptability to any size of congregation, and it can be tailored to local church tastes and worship styles, depending on the music selected for each segment.

Service One
Tenebrae
A Service of Darkness

ORGAN PRELUDE

SCRIPTURE MEDITATION

"For, behold, the darkness shall cover the earth, and gross darkness the people: but the LORD shall arise upon thee, and his glory shall be seen upon thee" (Isa. 60:2).

"And the light shineth in darkness; and the darkness comprehended it not" (John 1:5).

THE LAST SUPPER

Hymn: "According to Thy Gracious Word"

Scripture

The Last Supper

Pastoral meditation

Hymn: "Here at Thy Table, Lord"
Communion

GETHSEMANE
Scripture
Hymn: "'Tis Midnight"

THE DENIAL AND TRIAL
Scripture
Hymn: "Lead Me to Calvary" (vv. 1 and 4)

THE SUFFERING SERVANT
Responsive Reading
Hymn: "Just as I Am"

CHRIST SENTENCED
Scripture
Hymn: "O Sacred Head, Now Wounded"

ON THE WAY TO THE CROSS
Scripture
Duet: "Blessed Redeemer"

CRUCIFIXION
Scripture
Silent Prayer
Organ Meditation: "There Is a Fountain"

DISMISSAL
Please reverently preserve this hour of remembrance, and leave the church building in silence.

Ponder these things in your heart.

"And there was a darkness over all the earth . . . And the sun was darkened" (Luke 23:44-45).

Service Two
Tenebrae
A Service of Shadows

ORGAN PRELUDE AND SILENT PRAYERS

CHORAL MEDITATION
"O Come and Mourn with Me Awhile"

CONGREGATIONAL HYMN
"There Is a Green Hill Far Away"

PRAYER
The Lord's Prayer

SHADOWS OF HOLY WEEK

1. The Shadow of His Body Broken for Us
   Scripture: Matt. 26:26-29
   Hymn: "Bread of the World in Mercy Broken"
   The Eucharist
   Prayer of Thanksgiving

2. The Shadow of the Betrayal
   Scripture: Matt. 26:17-25
   Ensemble: "Ah, Holy Jesus"

3. The Servant
   Responsive Reading
   Hymn: "O Sacred Head, Now Wounded"
   Scripture: John 13:1-17

4. The Shadow of the Desertion
   Scripture: Matt. 26:31-35
   Hymn: "'Tis Midnight"

5. The Shadow of an Unshared Vigil
   Scripture: Matt. 26:36-45
   Hymn: "'Tis Midnight"

6. The Arrest at the Gate
   Scripture: John 18:1-5
   Ensemble: "Go to Dark Gethsemane"

7. The Shadow of the Cross
   Scripture: Mark 15:16-20
   Songs of the Cross
   Congregational medley

DARKNESS

Silence

THE RETURN OF THE LIGHT

BENEDICTION

DISMISSAL

Please leave the church in silence, allowing your heart to ponder these things.

A Word About This Service

The ancient Tenebrae service dates back to the early centuries of the Christian Church. Coming from the Latin word meaning "shadows," Tenebrae depicts the flight of the disciples and the approaching Crucifixion. It summarizes the events and teachings that occurred in Holy Week from Maundy Thursday and Good Friday, preparatory to the Resurrection on Easter Sunday.

As you enter, meditate that it was Maundy Thursday when the 12 disciples were with Jesus in the Upper Room for the last time, and that He and they stood in the shadow of the Cross.

The extinguishing of the candles and lights as the service progresses symbolizes the approaching hour of the Crucifixion. The time of total darkness recalls the hours Christ was in the tomb. The return of the light is prophetic of the Easter soon to dawn.

Think and pray on the meaning this service has for you and for the church.

Maundy Thursday Service

With Christ . . .
   At the feet of Peter
   At the Passover meal
   In the Garden of Gethsemane

SCRIPTURE FOR THE EVENING: John 13:1-17; Matt. 26:26-30; Matt. 26:36-50

WORSHIP LEADERS

ORDER OF SERVICE

ORGAN PRELUDE
   "O Sacred Head, Now Wounded" (tune: Hassler, arranged by Bach)

GREETING AND CALL TO WORSHIP
   Hymn: "There Is a Green Hill Far Away"

WITH CHRIST AT THE FEET OF PETER
   Scripture reading: John 13:1-17
   The meaning of "maundy"
   A prayer of application
   "Must Jesus Bear the Cross Alone?"

WITH CHRIST AT THE PASSOVER MEAL
   Scripture reading: Matt. 26:26-30
   The Passover meal and the Lord's Supper

Holy Communion
"Were You There?"

WITH CHRIST IN THE GARDEN OF GETHSEMANE
Scripture reading: Matt. 26:36-50
"'Tis Midnight"
Lest We Forget Gethsemane
Hymn: "Lead Me to Calvary"

BENEDICTION

ORGAN POSTLUDE
"Lift High the Cross"
"Let us go quietly . . ."

Pastor: O Lord, You who came to call sinners to repentance:

People: Call us still that we may answer.

Pastor: You who did meet the hardness of the thief:

People: Soften the hearts of all who are impenitent.

Pastor: You who did call Zacchaeus from the sycamore tree:

People: Arouse the careless and arrest the curious.

Pastor: You who did speak words of spirit and of life:

People: Enlighten the ignorant and teach the un-learned.

Pastor: Dispel all prejudice and correct all error:

People: Establish Your people in the truth of Your gospel.

Pastor: You who did pray for Your murderers:

People: Pity those who persecute Your servants.

Pastor: You who did call out many devils:

People: Set free by the power of Your grace the many who are victims of pride and anger, of greed and selfishness.

Pastor: You who did satisfy the doubts of Thomas:

People: Deal gently with those who can scarcely believe.

Pastor: You who did uplift the sinking Peter:

People: Support all who are weak and unstable.

Pastor: You who did proclaim deliverance to the captives:

People: Pity all prisoners and loose the bonds of their sin.

Pastor: You who did raise the dead to life:

People: Quicken us all to life in Your righteousness.

Pastor: You who did come to save Your people from their sins:

People: Save, O Lord, those who put their trust in You.

Easter Sunday Service

Welcome to the grandest day of celebration of the Church year—Easter Sunday! It is without a doubt a glorious day for us to gather to worship our risen Lord—the King of Kings and Lord of Lords, the Great High Priest of the Kingdom of Light. Come now into His presence in a spirit of jubilant celebration, proclaiming that He is risen indeed!

ORGAN PRELUDE

WE ARE CALLED TO CELEBRATE
In an Easter call to worship

CHOIR AND INSTRUMENTATION
"Christ Is Risen: Alleluia!"

WE CELEBRATE IN SONG
Hymn: "Christ, the Lord, Is Risen Today"
Youth handbells

Hymn: "Christ Arose"
Hymn: "Hallelujah! What a Savior!"

WE JOIN IN PRAYER

Pastoral prayer

Pastor

Welcome to God by the new and *living Way!*

OUR CELEBRATION CONTINUES

Through music: "All Glory, Laud, and Honor"

Youth handbells

As we fellowship

Pastor

As we give

Offertory

WE ARE MINISTERED TO

In song: "Great Is Jehovah the Lord" (from *How Great Thou Art,* written by Franz Schubert, arranged by David T. Clydesdale; sanctuary choir and instrumentation)

Through His servant: "The Light Breaks Forth—Victorious"

Pastor

WE RESPOND

In a prayer of benediction

Pastor

WE DEPART

Continuing to celebrate and worship the risen Christ

Lord's Day Morning

Let an atmosphere of worship begin with the organ prelude. Use these moments to enter privately into a spirit of prayer and praise.

ORGAN PRELUDE

CHORAL CALL TO WORSHIP
"Rejoice, the Lord Is King" (arranged by Fettke)

INVOCATION

CONGREGATIONAL HYMNS
"Christ, the Lord, Is Risen Today"
"Christ Arose"

SCRIPTURE READING
Matt. 28:1-7

PRAYER TIME

CHORAL CALL TO PRAYER
"Easter Prayer" (arranged by Fettke)

PASTORAL PRAYER
Congregational response: "Alleluia"

CHANCEL CHOIR AND BRASS
"Easter Fanfare" (by Jane Marshall)

FRIENDSHIP TIME

Pass the friendship register.

ANNOUNCEMENTS

WORSHIP THROUGH GIVING
  Organ offertory

VOCAL SOLO

MORNING MESSAGE
  "The Easter Imperatives" (Matt. 28:1-7)

CLOSING

BENEDICTION

CHORAL BENEDICTION
  "An Easter Benediction" (by Edwin M. Willmington)

ORGAN POSTLUDE

And Can It Be?
A Celebration of the Atonement

Palm Sunday Evening

ORGAN PRELUDE

"Carillon de Westminster" (Louis Vierne)

CONGREGATIONAL HYMN

"Arise, My Soul, Arise"

WELCOME AND INVOCATION

"And Can It Be?" (Ovid Young, arranger)

"God So Loved the World" (John Stainer)

"God Hath Provided a Lamb" (Linda Almond; Ronn Huff, arranger)

"Hallelujah" (Mount of Olives; Beethoven)

"The Blood Will Never Lose Its Power" (Andrae Crouch; Dick Bolks, arranger)

"When I Survey the Wondrous Cross" (Ovid Young, arranger)

FRIENDSHIP/ANNOUNCEMENTS/OFFERING

Organ offertory: "Wondrous Love" (Dale Wood)

"Christ Arose" (Ronn Huff, arranger)

"Christ, Be Thine the Glory" (Heinrich Shutz)

"Because He Lives" (William Gaither; Ronn Huff, arranger)

"We Shall Behold Him" (Dottie Rambo; Ronn Huff, arranger)

"Hallelujah" (*Messiah*, G. F. Handel)

BENEDICTION

CHORAL BENEDICTION

"The Lord Bless You and Keep You" (Lutkin)

ORGAN POSTLUDE

"Fanfare" (Francis Jackson)

A SERVICE OF HEALING

This service may be used in corporate worship, in the home or hospital room, in a prayer group meeting, or other appropriate setting. It is intended to express in both content and structure the confidence that God can and does heal, while it celebrates the reality that the ultimate hope of the Christian faith is not found in physical wellness but in the resurrection of the righteous.

GREETING AND PREPARATION

SCRIPTURE

Any one or more of the following scripture passages may serve as the foundation upon which a message may be built, or one or more of the passages may be read as scriptural warrant for the faith of the Church in God's attentiveness to the needs of His people.

2 Kings 5:1-19	Matt. 10:1-8
Ps. 13	Matt. 15:21-28
Ps. 23	Mark 5:24b-34
Ps. 27	Mark 10:46-52
Ps. 51:1-12, 15-17	Luke 5:17-26
Ps. 91	Luke 7:11-17
Ps. 103:1-5	Luke 17:11-19
Eccles. 3:1-11a	John 4:46-54
Isa. 35:1-10	John 5:2-18
Isa. 40:28-31	John 9

Isa. 43:1-3a, 18-19, 25	Acts 3:1-10
Isa. 53:3-5	Acts 5:12-16
Matt. 4:23-24	Rom. 8
Matt. 5:1-12	Rom. 14:7-12
Matt. 9:18-35	1 Cor. 12:4-11
2 Cor. 1:3-5	Heb. 12:1-2
2 Cor. 4:16-18	James 5:13-16
2 Cor. 12:7-10	1 John 5:13-15
Col. 1:11-29	Rev. 21:1-4

SERMON OR TESTIMONY

CONFESSION AND PARDON*

If James 5:13-20, or portions thereof, has not been read earlier in the service, it may be read as a call to confession to those whose hearts are hungry for redemption or for assurance and in preparation for anointing and prayer for healing.

The minister may lead in a prayer of confession and supplication, inviting those present to respond in confession and faith.

The Lord's Prayer

A hymn of response and praise may be sung.

HOLY COMMUNION*

The minister may administer Holy Communion to all present who wish to share in the Lord's table. The service may be adapted from the rituals suggested in this manual.

THANKSGIVING FOR THE OIL*

The minister may pray an extemporaneous prayer or may pray the following prayer:

Let us pray:

O God, Giver of salvation and ultimate Source of all healing, we give You thanks for the meaning of this symbol of Your presence. As Your disciples were sent to heal the sick and anoint them in Your name, so we today follow the admonition of Your Word to anoint with oil this our brother (sister).

Pour out Your Holy Spirit on us, that those who in faith and repentance receive this anointing may be made whole; through Jesus Christ our Lord. Amen.

HYMN OF HEALING

The following suggested hymns or songs may be used: "Be Still and Know," "Come, Holy Spirit," "He Touched Me," "Rise and Be Healed," "There Is a Balm in Gilead."

PRAYERS FOR HEALING AND WHOLENESS WITH ANOINTING AND/OR LAYING ON OF HANDS

People may be invited to come forward individually or as a group to the altar or other prayer area. They may express any specific concerns or needs, and the minister or other designated persons may pray for them.

If there is anointing with oil, the minister or other leader shall touch a thumb or finger to the oil and touch the person's forehead with it, in silence, or using one of the following:

_____, I anoint you with oil in the name of the Father and of the Son and of the Holy Spirit _____ (for specific need).

May the power of the risen Christ be in you, and may His Holy Spirit heal you of all illnesses—of body, mind, spirit, and relationships—that you may serve God with a ready heart and a loving spirit. Amen.

Or,

_____, I lay my hands upon you and anoint you in the name of the Father and of the Son and of the Holy Spirit, beseeching our Lord Jesus Christ to sustain you with His presence, to drive away all sickness of body and spirit, and to give you that victory of life and peace that will enable you to serve Him both now and forevermore. Amen.

The minister may then add:

As you are outwardly anointed with this oil, so may our Heavenly Father grant you an inward anointing with the Holy Spirit.

May He release you from suffering and restore you to wholeness and strength.

May He deliver you from all evil, preserve you in all goodness, and bring you to everlasting life; through Jesus Christ our Lord. Amen.

PRAYER AFTER ANOINTING

The following, or another suitable prayer, may be used:

Almighty God, we pray that _____ (our brothers and sisters) may be comforted in their suffering and made whole. Grant them courage and strength, patience and hope.

May Your peace sustain them now and so preserve their hope that whenever death may come, they may be assured of Your welcome and may be received into Your open arms.

In the name of Jesus Christ our Lord. Amen.

TESTIMONIES OF PRAISE AND THANKSGIVING

Those who desire to do so may give thanks to God for healing or other blessings.

HYMN OF PRAISE

BENEDICTION AND DISMISSAL

An Order for Anointing and Prayer for Healing

The following may be used within a worship service or other setting where the desire has been expressed for anointing with oil and prayer for healing.

At an appropriate time in the service, those desiring anointing and prayer for healing may be invited to the altar with the following invitation:

We come to this moment with a certainty in God's care for all the life of His people. The Lord Jesus Christ, while He ministered on earth, was often about the work of healing physical infirmities as well as touching the deeper needs of people.

At this time of prayer today, I invite _____ to come forward for anointing, along with any others who desire the grace of anointing to be administered. We join in responding to the admonition of the Word as it is expressed for us in James 5:7-18. Those who wish to join _____ in support of his (her) petition in prayer, please come and kneel with him (her).

> When the petitioner has come, along with any who desire to join with them, the minister may pray extempore or may use the following prayer:

O God, Giver of health and salvation: We cherish this oil as a symbol of Your presence with us, and as a reminder of Your interest in the whole of our existence spiritually, emotionally, and physically. As the holy apostles of Your Son, Jesus Christ, anointed many who were sick and healed them, so may those who in faith and repentance receive this holy unction be made whole; through Jesus Christ our Lord, who lives and reigns with You and with the Holy Spirit, one God, for ever and ever. Amen.

> The minister may then anoint those desiring it, touching the forehead of the petitioner with oil applied with the thumb or forefinger, and say:

I anoint you with oil in the name of the Father and of the Son and of the Holy Spirit, beseeching our Lord Jesus Christ to sustain you with His presence, to drive away all sickness of body and spirit, and to give you that victory of life and peace that will enable you to serve Him both now and evermore.

As you are outwardly anointed with this oil, so may the Father grant you the inward anointing of the Holy Spirit. May He forgive you your sins, release you from suffering, and restore you to wholeness and strength. May He deliver you from all evil, preserve you in all goodness, and bring you to everlasting life; through Jesus Christ our Lord. Amen.

A SERVICE OF RECONCILIATION

A service of reconciliation is intended for use in those cases when conflicts threaten to destroy the unity, harmony, and effectiveness of the Body of Christ. It should not be utilized for the minor or occasional differences that exist in churches or groups within the church that are the result of human frailty or differences caused by personality or preference.

The use of a Service of Reconciliation should be undertaken with the utmost caution and care. It should not be utilized too quickly, or with surface attempts to bridge over deep and underlying tensions that seriously divide people from one another, and which, unless resolved, may serve to do lasting harm to the offended parties, their families, and the witness of the Body of Christ.

This service is designed to culminate a series of intentional steps toward reconciliation. There should have been serious consultation with church leaders, fervent prayer, openness to the leadership of the Holy Spirit, careful searching of the Word for guidance, and an expressed desire on the part of all parties involved to seek reconciliation for the sake of the kingdom of God, the salvation of the lost, the sanctification of believers, and the effectiveness of the Church.

The leaders in the service should have consulted together and must have received the encouragement and participation of all parties in a dispute if a genuine reconciliation is to occur. The planning of the service should include participants in whatever conflict has threatened the fellowship. The service must be bathed in prayer, entered into with humility, and intended to bring to an end any enmity, strife, or ongoing alienation.

Suggested passages of scripture for background study include:

Gal. 5:1-26   Eph. 4:1—5:2   Phil. 4:2-9   Col. 3:1-17

The following service order is suggested for use:

GATHERING

Various hymns may be utilized for the gathering of the people in preparation for the service. Among them are: "My Faith Looks Up to Thee," "Have Thine Own Way, Lord," "Jesus Paid It All," "Nearer, Still Nearer," "Our Great Savior."

WE ACKNOWLEDGE THE DESIRES OF GOD

Reader 1: One of the teachers of the law came and heard them debating. Noticing that Jesus had given them a good answer, he asked him, "Of all the commandments, which is the most important?"

"The most important one," answered Jesus, "is this: 'Hear, O Israel, the Lord our God, the Lord is one. Love the Lord your God with all your heart and with all your soul and with all your mind and with all your strength.' The second is this: 'Love your neighbor as yourself.' There is no commandment greater than these."

"Well said, teacher," the man replied. "You are right in saying that God is one and there is no other but him. To love him with all your heart, with all your understanding and with all your strength, and to love your neighbor as yourself is more important than all burnt offerings and sacrifices."

When Jesus saw that he had answered wisely, he said to him, "You are not far from the kingdom of God" *(Mark 12:28-34, NIV).*

Reader 2: For this is the message you have heard from the beginning, that we should love one another. . . . We know that we have passed from death to life because we love one another. Whoever does not love abides in death. All who hate a brother or sister are murderers, and you know that murderers do not have eternal life abiding in them. We know love by this, that he laid down his life for us—and we ought to lay down our lives for one another. . . . Little children, let us love, not in word or speech, but in truth and action. . . . And this is his commandment, that we should believe in the name of his Son Jesus Christ and love one another, just as he has commanded us *(1 John 3:11, 14-16, 18, 23, NRSV).*

Reader 3: "A new command I give you: Love one another. As I have loved you, so you must love one another. By this all men will know that you are my disciples, if you love one another."

"As the Father has loved me, so have I loved you. Now remain in my love. If you obey my commands, you will remain in my love, just as I have obeyed my Father's commands and remain in his love. I have told you this so that my joy may be in you and that your joy may be complete. My command is this: Love each other as I have loved you. Greater love has no one than this, that he lay down his life for his friends. You are my friends if you do what I command. . . . You did not choose me, but I chose you and appointed you to go and bear fruit—fruit that will last. Then the Father will give you whatever you ask in my name. This is my command: Love each other" *(John 13:34-35; 15:9-14, 16-17, NIV)*.

WE ACKNOWLEDGE OUR NEED

> Individually (Each participant in the service is asked to read the following in silence, standing, kneeling at the altar or at the pew, or seated.)

Have mercy on me, O God, according to your unfailing love; according to your great compassion blot out my transgressions. Wash away all my iniquity and cleanse me from my sin. For I know my transgressions, and my sin is always before me. Against you, you only, have I sinned and done what is evil in your sight, so that you are proved right when you speak and justified when you judge.

Surely you desire truth in the inner parts; you teach me wisdom in the inmost place. Cleanse me . . . and I will be clean; wash me, and I will be whiter than snow.

Create in me a pure heart, O God, and renew a steadfast spirit within me. . . . A broken and contrite heart, O God, you will not despise *(Ps. 51:1-4, 6-7, 10, 17, NIV)*.

> Corporately

Unison: Almighty and merciful God, we know that when we offend another, we offend You. We are aware that we have often allowed the shadow of hate to cloud our souls, hiding the light from our unseeing eyes. We have said unpleasant and hurtful things to our brothers and sisters when they have failed to live up to our expectations. Grant that we might find that spark of love that ever burns within us, the love that You have shown us even when we failed You. Fan the embers of that love until it roars again in flames of love, peace, and reconciliation. Forgive us our sins and help us to forgive those who have sinned against us. Lead us into new life through Your Son Jesus Christ, who died for the sins of all. Amen.[22]

WE PRAY THE LORD'S PRAYER

SCRIPTURE

Therefore, as God's chosen people, holy and dearly loved, clothe yourselves with compassion, kindness, humility, gentleness and patience. Bear with each other and forgive whatever grievances you may have against one another. Forgive as the Lord forgave you. And over all these virtues put on love, which binds them all together in perfect unity.

Let the peace of Christ rule in your hearts, since as members of one body you were called to peace. And be thankful. Let the word of Christ dwell in you richly as you teach and admonish one another with all wisdom, and as you sing psalms, hymns and spiritual songs with gratitude in your hearts to God. And whatever you do, whether in word or deed, do it all in the name of the Lord Jesus, giving thanks to God the Father through him *(Col. 3:12-17, NIV)*.

WE GRANT TO ONE ANOTHER THE PARDON OF CHRIST

Leader: It is the awesome privilege and responsibility of the Body of Christ to embody the grace of God. We therefore extend to others the grace He has extended to each of us. As Jesus commissioned His disciples to announce forgiveness to the contrite and repentant, so we announce His forgiveness to one another.

People: In the peace of Christ, and on the basis of His grace alone, I extend to you the forgiveness of Christ. I release you from guilt before me and stand with you all as brothers and sisters in Him.

Leader: Having granted forgiveness, we may with joy receive it. Let us embrace the pardon extended to us.

People: I receive your forgiveness as freely as Christ has provided it to us all. We stand forgiven in Him. I embrace the pardon you have given me and will live my life in gratitude to God and to you.

Leader: Let us commit ourselves to the pursuit of purity of heart and life before God and one another that is pleasing to Him.

People: May God himself, the God of peace, sanctify us through and through. May our spirits and souls and bodies be kept sound and blameless at the coming of our Lord Jesus Christ. The one who calls us is faithful, and He will do this *(see 1 Thess. 5:23-24).*

WE CELEBRATE THE LORD'S SUPPER AS ONE

The administration of the Lord's Supper may be introduced by appropriate remarks or a brief homily and the reading of 1 Cor. 11:23-29; Luke 22:14-20; or some other suitable passage. Let the minister then give the following invitation:

The Lord himself ordained this holy sacrament. He commanded His disciples to partake of the bread and wine, emblems of His broken body and shed blood. This is His table. The feast is for His disciples. Let all those who have with true repentance forsaken their sins, and have believed in Christ unto salvation, draw near and take these emblems and, by faith, partake of the life of Jesus Christ, to your soul's comfort and joy. Let us remember that it is the memorial of the death and passion of our Lord; also a token of His coming again. Let us not forget that we are one, at one table with the Lord.

The minister may offer a prayer of confession and supplication, concluding with the following prayer of consecration:

Almighty God, who through Your tender mercy gave Your only Son, Jesus Christ, to suffer death upon the Cross for our redemption: hear us, we humbly pray. Grant that, as we receive these creatures of bread and wine according to the holy institution of Your Son, our Savior Jesus Christ, in remembrance of His passion and death, we may be made partakers of the benefits of His atoning sacrifice.

We are reminded that in the same night that our Lord was betrayed, He took bread and, when He had given thanks, He broke it and gave it to His disciples, saying, "This is my body given for you; do this in remembrance of me" (1 Cor. 11:24, NIV). Likewise, after supper, He took the cup, and when He had given thanks, He gave it to them, saying, "This cup is the new covenant in my blood, which is poured out for you (Luke 22:20, NIV); do this, whenever you drink it, in remembrance of me" (1 Cor. 11:25, NIV).

May we come before You in true humility and faith as we partake of this holy sacrament. Through Jesus Christ our Lord. Amen.

> Then may the minister, partaking first, with the assistance of any other ministers present and, when necessary, of the stewards, administer the Communion to the people.

> While the bread is being distributed, let the minister say:

The body of our Lord Jesus Christ, which was broken for you, preserve you blameless unto everlasting life. Take and eat this, in remembrance that Christ died for you.

> As the cup is being passed, let the minister say:

The blood of our Lord Jesus Christ, which was shed for you, preserve you blameless unto everlasting life.

Drink this, in remembrance that Christ's blood was shed for you, and be thankful.

After all have partaken, the minister may then offer a concluding prayer of thanksgiving and commitment.

BENEDICTION

JOHN WESLEY'S COVENANT SERVICE[23]

An Introduction

To John Wesley, founder of Methodism and principal human motivation behind the great revival that swept England and Wales in the 18th century, one means of "increasing serious religion" was the joining of believers in a covenant "to serve God with all our heart and with all our soul." He urges Methodists to renew, "at every point, our Covenant, that the Lord should be our God."

The word *covenant* has rich meaning throughout the Bible. (See Gen. 2:16-17; 6:18; 1 Sam. 18:3; Pss. 25:10; 103:18; Jer. 50:5; Matt. 26:28; Acts 3:25; Rom. 11:26-27; Heb. 7:22.) According to most contemporary dictionaries, *covenant* denotes a solemn and binding agreement; a contract; a promise between two or more parties.

When filtered through the light of God's Word and religious experience, the term *covenant* becomes a binding agreement between God and man, a promise that is dependent one upon the other. Throughout the Old Testament, and continuing into the New, God made a promise (a commitment) of continual life and favor to man on condition of obedience, coupled with a penalty for disobedience.

On August 11, 1755, John Wesley refers to an occasion when he conducted a service that provided opportunity for making or renewing individual covenants with God. At the close of that 6 P.M. meeting in the French Church in Spitalfields "all the people stood up, in testimony of assent, to the number of about 1,800 persons." The *Journal* entry closes with "such a night I scarce ever saw before. Surely the fruit of it shall remain for ever."

The success of this Covenant Service encouraged Wesley to have it published as a pamphlet in 1780. It was in this form that the service received wide distribution and use for nearly a century.

As the Church has come to recognize the value of greater congregational involvement and participation in public worship, the need for providing meaningful opportunities for making and expressing one's personal covenant relationship with God has come to the forefront. Such a need resulted in the rediscovery, by churches of varied worship traditions, of the beauty and scriptural authority contained in Wesley's original Covenant Service.

This abridged and edited version is closely based on the spirit and text of the 1780 version. It retains much of the author's language, but it veers from the original in that it suggests specific hymn selections, which are found in this volume.

To all who participate in a worship service based on this material, or who make use of it for personal devotional reading, may this historical connection with the Wesleyan Church and teaching be a reminder of our natural condition as sinners and our responsibility to reaffirm a personal covenant relationship with God. It should also provide for a renewed realization of God's promises and presence.

Suggested Use of the Covenant Service

It was John Wesley's traditional practice to make use of the Covenant Service for Watch Night or on the first Sunday of the year. These continue to be viable options. Churches may also wish to consider using it on what has become Aldersgate

Sunday in Methodist churches. Isolated portions may be selected for use in other contexts, such as for reading or congregational meditation, and there is a wealth of material here for private devotional use.

For some modern worshipers, especially those of the evangelical and nonliturgical tradition, such a structured service may at first appear to be a hindrance to true worship; but as the scriptural allusions are understood, hymns sung within the context of the service, prayers prayed earnestly, and the minister's exhortations delivered with personal conviction and unction, there will be an awareness on the part of the participants of the value of this traditional service. It will be beneficial to print all portions of the service, except for the minister's exhortation, in the worship folder.

The Service

INSTRUMENTAL PRELUDE

Minister: "Come, let us join ourselves to the LORD in an everlasting covenant which will never be forgotten" (Jer. 50:5, RSV).

HYMN: "Rejoice, the Lord Is King"

Minister: Almighty God, unto whom all hearts are open, all desires known, and from whom no secrets are hid; cleanse the thoughts of our hearts by the inspiration of Thy Holy Spirit, that we may perfectly love Thee, and worthily magnify Thy holy name through Christ our Lord. Amen.

Then shall follow the minister and people praying together.

Minister and People: The Lord's Prayer (Matt. 6:9-13) (Use "trespasses")

THE SCRIPTURE LESSON: John 15:1-8

HYMN: "Jesus, We Look to Thee"

Minister: My dear friends, get these three principles fixed in your hearts: that things eternal are much more substantial than things temporal; that things not seen are as certain as the things that are seen; that upon your present choice depends your eternal lot. Choose Christ and His ways, and you are blessed forever; refuse, and you are undone forever.

And then, beloved, make your choice. Turn either to the right hand or to the left; Christ with His yoke, His cross, and His crown; or the devil with his wealth, his pleasure, and his curse. Then ask yourselves, "Soul, you see what is before you; what will you do? Which will you have, either the crown or the curse? If you choose the crown, remember that the day you take this, you must be content to submit to the cross and yoke, the service and sufferings of Christ, which are linked to it. What do you say? Had you rather take the gains and pleasures of sin and risk the curse? Or will you yield yourself a servant to Christ and so make sure the crown?"

Do not delay the matter. If you are unresolved, you

are resolved: if you remain undetermined for Christ, you are determined for the devil. Therefore follow your hearts from day to day; let them not rest till the matter be brought to an issue, and see that you make a good choice.

Next, embark with Christ. Adventure yourselves with Him. Cast yourselves upon His righteousness. You are exiles from the presence of God and fallen into a land of robbers and murderers. Your sins are robbers, your pleasures are robbers, your companions in sin are robbers and thieves. If you stay where you are, you perish. Christ offers, if you will venture with Him, to bring you to God. Will you say now to Him, "Lord Jesus, wilt Thou undertake for me? Wilt Thou bring me to God and bring me into the land of promise? With Thee I will venture myself. I cast myself upon Thee, upon Thy blood, upon Thy righteousness."

This is coming to Christ as your Priest. And by this you now renounce your own righteousness.

Do you deeply sense your sins and misery without Christ?

CONFESSION

People: We acknowledge a deep sense of sin and misery. We see ourselves as sinners in need of a Savior. The Spirit of God has awakened us; a kind of awakening, as it were, in hell. We cry,

"Lord, what am I! What mean these legions round about me? These chains and fetters that are upon me?

"Lord, where am I! Is there no hope of escaping out of this wretched state? I am but dead, if I continue as I am. What may I do to be saved?"

Minister: Being made sensible of his sin and his danger, a sinner will look for help and deliverance, but he will look everywhere else before he looks unto Christ. Nothing will bring a sinner to Christ but absolute necessity. He will try to forsake his sins. He will go to prayers and sermons and sacraments, and search out if there be salvation in them. But all these, though they be useful in their places, are of no help. His duties cannot help him; these may be reckoned among his sins. Ordinances cannot help; these are but empty cisterns. They all tell him, "You knock at a wrong door; salvation is not in us."

Do you now utterly despair of your own goodness, or do you trust in anything but Christ?

SUPPLICATION

People: Lord, be merciful to me. What shall I do? Abide as I am I dare not, and how to help myself I know not. My praying will not help me. My hearing will not help me. If I give all my goods to the poor, if I should give my body to be burned, all this would not save my soul. Woe is me. What shall I do?

Minister: You must let your sins go. You must let your righteousness go. Christ came not to call the righteous, but sinners to repentance. He came to seek and to save them that are lost.

Friends, will you now adventure on Christ? You have this threefold assurance:

First, God's ordination. Christ is He whom God the Father hath appointed and sent into the world to save sinners. This is He whom God the Father has sealed as the Savior who is redeeming and reconciling the world to himself.

Second, God's command. This is His commandment, that we should believe on the name of His Son, Jesus Christ.

Third, the promise of God. "Behold, I lay in Sion a chief corner stone, elect, precious: and he that believeth on him shall not be confounded" (1 Pet. 2:6).

Now, having this threefold assurance of God's ordinance, command, and promise, you may now be bold to adventure on Christ and to apply yourselves to Him.

Then shall follow the minister and people praying together.

Minister and People: Lord Jesus, here I am, a lost creature, an enemy to God, under His wrath and curse. Wilt Thou, Lord, undertake for me, reconcile me to God, and save my soul? Do not, Lord, refuse me, for if Thou refuse me, to whom then shall I go?

If I had come in my own name, Thou mightest well

have put me back; but since I come at the command of the Father, reject me not. Lord, help me. Lord, save me.

I come, Lord. I believe, Lord. I throw myself upon Thy grace and mercy. I cast myself upon Thy blood. Do not refuse me. I have not whither else to go. Here I will stay. On Thee I will trust and rest and venture myself. On Thee I lay my hope for pardon, for life, for salvation. If I perish, I perish on Thy shoulders. If I sink, I sink in Thy vessel. If I die, I die at Thy door. Bid me not go away, for I will not go.

COMMITMENT

Minister: Yield yourselves now to the Lord. As His servants, give up the dominion and government of yourselves to Christ. "Neither yield ye your members as instruments of unrighteousness unto sin: but yield yourselves unto God, as those that are alive from the dead, and your members as instruments of righteousness unto God." "To whom ye yield yourselves servants to obey, his servants ye are to whom ye obey" (Rom. 6:13, 16). Yield yourselves so to the Lord that you may henceforth be the Lord's.

Those that yield themselves to sin and the world, their hearts say, "Sin, I am yours; World, I am yours; Riches, I am yours; Pleasures, I am yours."

Rather, with the psalmist, we say to the Lord.

Then shall minister and people affirm together.

Minister and People: I am Thine; I reverence Thee. I dedicate myself to Thy service.

Minister: In so giving yourselves to the Lord, you affirm that you will be heartily contented that He appoint you to your work.

Let Him appoint you to your work. Christ has many services to be done; some are more easy and honorable, others more difficult and menial.

Some are suitable to our inclinations and interest; others are contrary to both. In some, we may please Christ and please ourselves, as when He requires us to feed and clothe ourselves. Indeed, there are some spiritual duties that are more pleasing than others; as to rejoice in the Lord, to be blessing and praising of God. These are the sweet works of a Christian. But then there are other works, wherein we cannot please Christ but by denying ourselves, as in bearing and forbearing, reproving men for their sins, withdrawing from their company; witnessing against their wickedness; confessing Christ and His name, when it will cost us shame and reproach; sailing against the wind, swimming against the tide, parting with our liberties and accommodations for the name of our Lord Jesus Christ.

See what it is that Christ expects and then yield yourselves to His whole will. Do not think of making your own terms with Christ; that will never be allowed you. Let us now approach Christ in prayer.

The people will join the minister in praying.

Minister and People: Lord Jesus, if Thou wilt receive me into Thy house, if Thou wilt but own me as Thy servant, I will not stand upon terms. Impose on me what condition Thou pleasest; write down Thy own articles; command me what Thou wilt; let me be Thy servant.

Make me what Thou wilt, Lord, and set me where Thou wilt. Let me be a vessel of silver or gold, or a vessel of wood or stone; so I be a vessel of honor. I am content. If I be not the head or the eye or the ear, one of the nobler and more honorable instruments Thou wilt employ, let me be the hand or the foot, as one of the lowest and least esteemed of all the servants of my Lord.

Minister: Lord, put me to what Thou wilt; rank me with whom Thou wilt.

People: Put me to doing; put me to suffering.

Minister: Let me be employed for Thee, or laid aside for Thee, exalted for Thee, or trodden under foot for Thee.

People: Let me be full; let me be empty.

Minister: Let me have all things; let me have nothing.

People: I freely and heartily resign all to Thy pleasure and disposal.

HYMN: "Lord, in the Strength of Grace"

Minister: Beloved, such a commitment to Christ as you have now made is that wherein the essence of Christianity lies. When you have chosen God to be your portion and happiness; when you have laid all your hopes upon Christ, casting yourself wholly upon the merits of His righteousness; when you have understandingly and heartily resigned and given up yourselves to Him; then you are Christians indeed, and never till then. Christ will be the Savior of none but of His servants. He is the Author of eternal salvation to those who obey Him. Christ will have no servants but by consent. His people are a willing people, and Christ will accept of no consent but in full to all that He requires. He will be all in all, or He will be nothing.

THE COVENANT

Minister: And now let us confirm our commitment by a solemn covenant, beginning with the singing of a covenant hymn.

HYMN: "Come, Let Us Use the Grace Divine"

Minister: Search your hearts whether you either have already or can now freely make this commitment to God in Christ. First, consider what your sins are and examine whether you can resolve to forego them all. Consider what the laws are, how holy, strict, and spiritual, and whether you can, upon deliberation, make choice of them all as the rule of your whole life.

Second, compose your spirits into the most serious frame possible, suitable to a transaction of so high importance.

Third, lay hold on the covenant of God and rely upon His promise of giving grace and strength, whereby you may be enabled to perform your promise. Trust not to your own strength, but take hold on His strength.

Fourth, resolve to be faithful. Having engaged your hearts, opened your mouths, and subscribed with your hands to the Lord, resolve in His strength never to go back.

Last, being thus prepared, in the most solemn manner possible, as if the Lord were visibly present before your eyes, bow and open your hearts to the Lord.

The minister and people will bow and pray together.

Minister and People: O most holy God, I beseech Thee, accept the poor prodigal prostrating himself at Thy door. I have fallen from Thee by my iniquity and am by nature a son of death and a thousandfold more the child of hell by my wicked practice. But of Thy infinite grace Thou hast promised mercy to me in Christ if I will but turn to Thee with all my heart. Therefore upon the call of Thy gospel, I am now come and, throwing down my weapons, submit myself to Thy mercy.

And because Thou requirest, as the condition of my peace with Thee, that I should put away my idols and be at defiance with all Thy enemies, I here from the bottom of my heart renounce them all. I firmly covenant with Thee not to allow myself in any known sin, but conscientiously to use all the means that I know Thou hast prescribed, for the death and utter destruction of all my corruptions. I humbly affirm before Thy glorious Majesty that it is the firm resolution of my heart to forsake all that is dear unto me in this world, rather than to turn from Thee to the ways of sin. I will watch against all its temptations, whether of prosperity or adversity, lest they should withdraw my heart from Thee.

And since Thou hast, of Thy boundless mercy, offered graciously to me to be my God through Christ, I call heaven and earth to record this day, that I do here solemnly acknowledge Thee as the Lord my God. I do here take Thee, the Lord Jehovah, Father, Son, and Holy Ghost, for my portion and do give up myself, body and soul, for Thy servant, promising and vowing to serve Thee in holiness and righteousness all the days of my life.

O blessed Jesus, I come to Thee hungry, wretched, miserable, blind, and naked, unworthy to wash the feet of the servants of my Lord, much less to be solemnly married to the King of Glory. But since such is Thy unparalleled love, I do here with all my power accept Thee and take Thee for my Head and Husband, to love, honor, and obey Thee before all others, and this to the death. I renounce my own worthiness and do here avow Thee for the Lord my righteousness. I renounce my own wisdom and do here take Thee for my only Guide. I renounce my own will and take Thy will for my law.

And since Thou hast told me I must suffer if I will reign, I do here covenant with Thee to take my lot, as it falls, with Thee and by Thy grace to run all hazards with Thee, purposing that neither life nor death shall part between Thee and me.

Now, Almighty God, Searcher of Hearts, Thou knowest that I make this covenant with Thee this day, without any known guile or reservation, beseeching Thee that if Thou seest any flaw or falsehood therein, Thou wouldst reveal it to me and help me to put it right.

HYMN: "Father, Son, and Holy Ghost"

All shall stand and say:

Minister and People: And now, glory be to Thee, O God the Father, whom I shall be bold from this day forward to look upon as my God and Father. Glory be to Thee, O God the Son, who hast loved me and washed me from my sins in Thy own blood and art now become my Savior and Redeemer. Glory be to Thee, O God the Holy Ghost, who by Thy almighty power has turned my heart from sin to God.

O eternal Jehovah, the Lord God Omnipotent, Father, Son, and Holy Ghost, Thou art now become my Covenant-Friend, and I, through Thy infinite grace, am become Thy Covenant-Servant. And the Covenant which I have made on earth, let it be ratified in heaven. Amen.

Now may follow the Holy Communion, or a hymn may be sung and the benediction given.

OPTIONAL HYMN: "Ye Servants of God"

CALLS TO WORSHIP
AND BENEDICTIONS[24]

Biblical Calls to Worship

New International Version

"Love the LORD, all his saints! The LORD preserves the faithful. . . . Be strong and take heart, all you who hope in the LORD" (Ps. 31:23-24, all NIV).

"I will extol the LORD at all times; his praise will always be on my lips. My soul will boast in the LORD; let the afflicted hear and rejoice. Glorify the LORD with me; let us exalt his name together" (Ps. 34:1-3).

"Who, O God, is like you? . . . I will praise you . . . for your faithfulness, O my God; I will sing praise to you . . . I, whom you have redeemed. My tongue will tell of your righteous acts all day long" (Ps. 71:19, 22-24).

"Come, let us sing for joy to the LORD. . . . Let us come before him with thanksgiving and extol him with music and song. . . . Come, let us bow down in worship, let us kneel before the LORD our Maker" (Ps. 95:1-2, 6).

"Sing to the LORD a new song, for he has done marvelous things. . . . Shout for joy to the LORD, all the earth, burst into jubilant song with music . . . and the sound of singing" (Ps. 98:1, 4-5).

"Shout for joy to the LORD, all the earth. Worship the LORD with gladness; come before him with joyful songs. . . . Enter his gates with thanksgiving . . . and praise his name" (Ps. 100:1-2, 4).

"Praise the LORD . . . and forget not all his benefits— who forgives all your sins and heals all your diseases . . . who satisfies your desires with good things so that your youth is renewed like the eagle's. . . . The LORD is compassionate and gracious. . . . From everlasting to everlasting the LORD's love is with those who fear him. . . . Praise the LORD" (Ps. 103:2-3, 5, 8, 17, 22).

"Praise the LORD. . . . I will praise the LORD all my life; I will sing praise to my God as long as I live. . . . Blessed is he . . . whose hope is in the LORD his God, . . . the LORD, who remains faithful forever" (Ps. 146:1-2, 5-6).

"Praise the LORD. Praise God in his sanctuary. . . . Praise him for his acts of power. . . . Praise him with . . . the trumpet, praise him with the harp and lyre. . . . Let everything that has breath praise the LORD" (Ps. 150:1-3, 6).

Biblical Benedictions and Blessings

A. *New International Version*

"May the LORD keep watch between you and me when we are away from each other" (Gen. 31:49).

"The LORD bless you and keep you; the LORD make his face shine upon you and be gracious to you; the LORD turn his face toward you and give you peace" (Num. 6:24-26).

"Love the LORD your God . . . walk in all his ways . . . obey his commands . . . hold fast to him . . . serve him with all your heart and all your soul" (Josh. 22:5).

"Praise be to the LORD, the God of Israel, from everlasting to everlasting. Amen and Amen" (Ps. 41:13).

"Praise be to the LORD God, the God of Israel, who alone does marvelous deeds. Praise be to his glorious name forever; may the whole earth be filled with his glory. Amen and Amen" (Ps. 72:18-19).

"Praise be to the LORD forever! Amen and Amen" (Ps. 89:52).

"Praise be to the LORD, the God of Israel, from everlasting to everlasting. Let all the people say, 'Amen!' Praise the LORD" (Ps. 106:48).

"Therefore go and make disciples . . . baptizing them in the name of the Father and of the Son and of the Holy Spirit, and teaching them to obey everything [Jesus has] commanded you" (Matt. 28:19-20).

"Grace and peace to you from God our Father and from the Lord Jesus Christ" (Rom. 1:7).

"Oh, the depth of the riches of the wisdom and knowledge of God! How unsearchable his judgments, and his paths beyond tracing out! . . . For from him and through him and to him are all things. To him be the glory forever! Amen" (Rom. 11:33, 36).

"For us there is but one God, the Father, from whom all things came and for whom we live; and there is but one Lord, Jesus Christ, through whom all things came and through whom we live" (1 Cor. 8:6).

"Praise be to the God and Father of our Lord Jesus Christ, the Father of compassion and the God of all comfort, who comforts us in all our troubles, so that we can comfort those in any trouble with the comfort we ourselves have received from God" (2 Cor. 1:3-4).

"May the grace of the Lord Jesus Christ, and the love of God, and the fellowship of the Holy Spirit be with you all" (2 Cor. 13:14).

"Grace and peace to you from God our Father and the Lord Jesus Christ, who gave himself for our sins to rescue us from the present evil age, according to the will of our God and Father, to whom be glory for ever and ever. Amen" (Gal. 1:3-5).

"Carry each other's burdens, and in this way you will fulfill the law of Christ. . . . Therefore, as we have opportunity, let us do good to all people, especially to those who belong to the family of believers" (Gal. 6:2, 10).

"The grace of our Lord Jesus Christ be with your spirit, brothers. Amen" (Gal. 6:18).

"Grace and peace to you from God our Father and the Lord Jesus Christ" (Eph. 1:2).

"Now to him who is able to do immeasurably more than all we ask or imagine, according to his power that is at work within us, to him be glory in the church and in Christ Jesus throughout all generations, for ever and ever! Amen" (Eph. 3:20-21).

"Peace to the brothers, and love with faith from God the Father and the Lord Jesus Christ. Grace to all who love our Lord Jesus Christ with an undying love" (Eph. 6:23-24).

"And [may] the peace of God, which transcends all understanding, . . . guard your hearts and your minds in Christ Jesus" (Phil. 4:7).

"To our God and Father be glory for ever and ever. Amen" (Phil. 4:20).

"The grace of the Lord Jesus Christ be with your spirit. Amen" (Phil. 4:23).

"May the Lord make your love increase and overflow for each other and for everyone else, just as ours does for you. May he strengthen your hearts so that you will be blameless and holy in the presence of our God and Father when our Lord Jesus comes with all his holy ones" (1 Thess. 3:12-13).

"May God himself, the God of peace, sanctify you through and through. May your whole spirit, soul and body be kept blameless at the coming of our Lord Jesus Christ. . . . The grace of our Lord Jesus Christ be with you" (1 Thess. 5:23, 28).

"May our Lord Jesus Christ himself and God our Father, who loved us and by his grace gave us eternal encouragement and good hope, encourage your hearts and strengthen you in every good deed and word" (2 Thess. 2:16-17).

"May the Lord direct your hearts into God's love and Christ's perseverance" (2 Thess. 3:5).

"Grace, mercy and peace from God the Father and Christ Jesus our Lord" (1 Tim. 1:2).

"Now to the King eternal, immortal, invisible, the only God, be honor and glory for ever and ever. Amen" (1 Tim. 1:17).

"Grace and peace from God the Father and Christ Jesus our Savior" (Titus 1:4).

"And the God of all grace, who called you to his eternal glory in Christ, after you have suffered a little while, will himself restore you and make you strong, firm and steadfast. To him be the power for ever and ever. Amen" (1 Pet. 5:10-11).

"Grace and peace be yours in abundance through the knowledge of God and of Jesus our Lord" (2 Pet. 1:2).

"To the only God our Savior be glory, majesty, power and authority, through Jesus Christ our Lord, before all ages, now and forevermore! Amen" (Jude 25).

"Worthy is the Lamb, who was slain, to receive power and wealth and wisdom and strength and honor and glory and praise! . . . To him who sits on the throne and to the Lamb be praise and honor and glory and power, for ever and ever! . . . Amen" (Rev. 5:12-14).

B. *King James Version*

"The LORD our God be with us, as he was with our fathers: let him not leave us, nor forsake us: that he may incline our hearts unto him, to walk in all his ways, and to keep his commandments, and his statutes, and his judgments, which he commanded our fathers" (1 Kings 8:57-58).

"Let the words of my mouth, and the meditation of my heart, be acceptable in thy sight, O LORD, my strength, and my redeemer" (Ps. 19:14).

"Now the God of hope fill you with all joy and peace in believing, that ye may abound in hope, through the power of the Holy Ghost. . . . Now the God of peace be with you all. Amen" (Rom. 15:13, 33).

"The grace of our Lord Jesus Christ be with you all. Amen" (Rom. 16:24).

"Now to him that is of power to stablish you according to my gospel, and the preaching of Jesus Christ, according to the revelation of the mystery, which was kept secret since the world began, but now is made manifest, and by the scriptures of the prophets, according to the commandment of the everlasting God, made known to all nations for the obedience of faith: to God only wise, be glory through Jesus Christ for ever. Amen" (Rom. 16:25-27).

"Grace be unto you, and peace, from God our Father, and from the Lord Jesus Christ" (1 Cor. 1:3).

"Be perfect, be of good comfort, be of one mind, live in peace; and the God of love and peace shall be with you. . . . The grace of the Lord Jesus Christ, and the love of God, and the communion of the Holy [Spirit], be with you all. Amen" (2 Cor. 13:11, 14).

"Peace be to the brethren, and love with faith, from God the Father and the Lord Jesus Christ. Grace be with all them that love our Lord Jesus Christ in sincerity. Amen" (Eph. 6:23-24).

"Wherefore also we pray always for you, that our God would count you worthy of this calling, and fulfill all the good pleasure of his goodness, and the work of faith with power: that the name of our Lord Jesus Christ may be glorified in you, and ye in him, according to the grace of our God and the Lord Jesus Christ" (2 Thess. 1:11-12).

"Now the Lord of peace himself give you peace always by all means. The Lord be with you all. . . . The grace of our Lord Jesus Christ be with you all. Amen" (2 Thess. 3:16, 18).

"Now the God of peace, that brought again from the dead our Lord Jesus, that great shepherd of the sheep, through the blood of the everlasting covenant, make you perfect in every good work to do his will, working in you that which is wellpleasing in his sight, through Jesus Christ; to whom be glory for ever and ever. Amen" (Heb. 13:20-21).

"Grace be with you, mercy, and peace, from God the Father, and from the Lord Jesus Christ, the Son of the Father, in truth and love" (2 John 3).

"Now unto him that is able to keep you from falling, and to present you faultless before the presence of his glory with exceeding joy, to the only wise God our Saviour, be glory and majesty, dominion and power, both now and ever. Amen" (Jude 24-25).

"Grace be unto you, and peace, from him which is, and which was, and which is to come; and from the seven Spirits which are before his throne; and from Jesus Christ, who is the faithful witness, and the first begotten of the dead, and the prince of the kings of the earth. Unto him that loved us, and washed us from our sins in his own blood, and hath made us kings and priests unto God and his Father; to him be glory and dominion for ever and ever. Amen" (Rev. 1:4-6).

Other Benedictions

Now may you continue to grow in the grace and knowledge of our Lord Jesus Christ, feeding on His Word, breathing in His Spirit, walking in His light, resting on His promises.

May His Spirit dwell within you, His Word abide in you, His will guide you, His joy strengthen you as you give Him your lives in loving service. Amen.

Go in peace. May you be constantly comforted by the thought that God loves you and wants you to be like Him through the power of the Holy Spirit. Amen.

Unto God's gracious mercy and protection we commit you; the Lord look upon you with His favor and fill you with all spiritual benediction and peace; that in this life, and in the world to come, you may be partakers of eternal grace, through Jesus Christ our Lord.

Go in peace; sin no more. Love one another.

May the same Spirit that settled upon the 120 on the Day of Pentecost energize you as you leave this church to serve in the world. Amen.

Lean thine arms upon the windowsill of heaven and gaze upon the Lord—then go out to meet thy day.

OFFERTORY IDEAS AND PRAYERS[25]

1. OFFERTORY IDEA

A senator's wife went into the ham business—no pun intended. She borrowed $100,000 for capital from a trust company. The business finally made $3 million in annual sales.

The chairman of the trust company said to the senator, "I'm glad the ham venture is doing well."

The senator asked, "What makes you think it's doing well?"

The chairman replied, "You used to call it 'Betty's business.' Now you call it 'our business.'"

That's not far off from church business. Nontithers call it "their church." Tithers lovingly refer to it as "our church."

Offertory Prayer

DEAR FATHER: Grant us grace to heed the word of praise or warning from Your Son: "Where your treasure is, there will your heart be also." In Jesus' name, Amen.

2. OFFERTORY IDEA

A pastor was speaking to the Sunday School about the things money can't buy. "It can't buy laughter, and it can't buy love," he told them. Driving his point home, he said, "What would you do if I offered you $1,000 not to love your mother and father?"

Stunned silence followed. Finally, a small voice asked, "How much would you give me not to love my big sister?"

Giving is not loving, but we can't love without giving!

Offertory Prayer

DEAR FATHER: We've discovered that Christian growth does not come by pouring in but by giving out! Accept our gifts of love. In Jesus' name, Amen.

3. OFFERTORY IDEA

An old radio recording of Amos 'n' Andy had an interesting conversation. Amos 'n' Andy were talking about finance.

Amos said to Andy: "Andy, if you got money, you can do business. If you don't, you gotta make arrangements."

Tithing is the best financial arrangement God has set up for developing Christian character and opportunities for learning to depend on Him.

Offertory Prayer

DEAR FATHER:

> *The more we give, the more we get;*
> *The more we laugh, the less we fret;*
> *The more we do unselfishly,*
> *The more we love abundantly;*
> *The more of everything we share,*

The more we show how much we care;
The more we love, the more we'll find
That life is good and friends are kind;
For only what we give away
Enriches us from day to day.
In Jesus' name, Amen.

4. OFFERTORY IDEA

It's been said in these economic times that the way to stay in the black today is to make and sell red ink.

Said the robin to the sparrow, "I should really like to know

Why these anxious human beings rush about and worry so."

Said the sparrow to the robin, "Friend, I think that it must be

That they have no Heavenly Father such as cares for you and me."

Offertory Prayer

DEAR FATHER: Please remind us that our individual stewardship is what we do after we have said, "I believe." In Jesus' name, Amen.

5. OFFERTORY IDEA

A writer was attempting to reconstruct the life of the Duke of Wellington in order to write a biography. The author said he learned most by finding an old account book of Wellington's. From it he learned how the great man spent his money.

The researcher thought the old account book of Wellington's spending taught him more about the man than reading speeches about the duke or even his own public pronouncements.

The way a man spends his money indicates what he thinks is important in life.

Offertory Prayer

> *Not what I get, but what I give—*
> *This be the gauge by which I live.*
> *Not merely joys that come my way,*
> *But the help I give to those astray.*
> *Not the rewards of money and fame,*
> *But the loads I lift in Jesus' name.*
> *This be the pay at the end of the day—*
> *Not what I keep, but give away.*
>
> In Jesus' name, Amen.

6. OFFERTORY IDEA

A state senator from Pennsylvania argued that his constituents were so drained financially, they simply could not afford to pay another cent in taxes.

In his oratory, he cited a letter from an irate voter as proof. The citizen had written him to protest higher taxes, insisting their family could not possibly pay any more. In fact, she pointed out, they already paid the government income taxes and sales taxes—and besides, they bought licenses for their two cars, summer camper, houseboat, and motorboat!

I wonder if that's how we sometimes sound to God when we declare we just can't afford to obey Him by tithing our income. I doubt God laughs about it.

Offertory Prayer
> *We mustn't boast how much we are giving*
> > *Until we've given Your part.*
> *Our tithe comes out of our wallet;*
> > *Our offering comes from our heart.*

> In Jesus' name, Amen.

7. OFFERTORY IDEA

A young woman was selling tickets for an upcoming charity concert. She had approached a well-known man of the community about buying some tickets for the charity event.

Politely but firmly he replied, "I'm sorry, but I won't be able to attend the concert. I know it's for a worthy cause. However, I'll assure you I shall be with you in spirit."

The young woman brilliantly exclaimed, "Fine! And where would you like to have your spirit sit? In the $5 section or the $10 section?"

Meekly, the gentleman replied: "I'll take a $10 ticket, please."

Now I know we are entering into the summer vacation season. I expect you all to get a good vacation away from responsibilities and pressure. I know you'll be with us in spirit!

And don't forget to have your spirit tithe regularly while you are on vacation.

Offertory Prayer

DEAR JESUS: We learned an important lesson by Your example: Worship without sacrifice is an impossibility! Amen.

8. OFFERTORY IDEA

The parish priest of Moncontour, France, looked at the meager offering in the collection plate. The coins didn't even cover the bottom.

The priest turned to his congregation and declared, "My brothers and sisters, earlier today, when I arrived at church, I saw all those fine cars parked in the square. I asked myself, Where are the poor? Now, having seen the collection basket, I wonder, Where are the rich?"

We'll find it better to be rich in God's eyes than rich in men's eyes. Men count dollars; God checks percentages! He asks 10 percent for the privilege of stewardship.

Offertory Prayer

DEAR HEAVENLY FATHER: We speak about stewardship—yet we know we should talk more about Lordship. When we are right on the Lordship of Jesus, we'll be right in our stewardship. Our pocketbooks will fall in line when we really learn that we are not our own but have been bought with a price! In Jesus' name, Amen.

9. OFFERTORY IDEA

Two preachers were discussing the financial situation of their churches. The holiness preacher, whose congregation numbered about 100, mentioned the amount of total giving by his church for the past year.

The other, pastor of a liberal church that ran three Sunday morning services totaling around 900, was astounded. The flabbergasted minister stated, "Your little church takes in more money than my big church!" Wistfully he added, "If it weren't for the bingo parties, our church would never make it. How do you people do it?"

The simple reply, "My people practice tithing!"

Tithing is the Bible method of support and the Bible method of developing strong, obedient stewards whom God can bless!

Offertory Prayer

DEAR HEAVENLY FATHER: Help us give according to our incomes, lest You make our incomes match our gifts! In Jesus' name, Amen.

10. OFFERTORY IDEA

One summer Monday night, I got to attend the opening exhibition game of the Los Angeles Rams in Anaheim Stadium. They played against—and lost to—the New England Patriots.

Standing in line to get a supper of Coke and a very dry hot dog, I heard a lot of grumbling from the patrons of the Rams. People who had good seats at the Coliseum for

243

more than 30 years had been assigned poor seats in Anaheim. That set up a mood of complaint. Many said they were going to quit going to the Rams' football games.

Here are some of the reasons given for staying home:

(1) The stadium has gotten so large that I don't see any of the old-time fans anymore. No one ever speaks to me.

(2) Game day is the only day I have to sleep.

(3) Often we have guests—and then other times we go to the cabin.

(4) The seats are hard.

(5) The coach never comes to call on me. He doesn't even recognize me on the street.

(6) The band and the cheerleaders use new tunes and yells. I like the old pep tunes better.

(7) There are some people in the stands who are hypocrites. Most of them just come to be seen by the TV cameras.

(8) I saw too many games as a child. My parents forced me to go.

(9) I can watch on TV without getting involved.

(10) They always have their hands out for money. I have to pay for a ticket every time I come.

Offertory Prayer

DEAR FATHER: In Your Book we discover a consistent principle: No one is really consecrated until his or her money is dedicated. In Jesus' name, Amen.

11. OFFERTORY IDEAS

Someone gave me a cartoon from *Family Circus*. Several little children were seated on stools and the floor, one boy was standing up on a low table with a book in hand, and a little girl had pulled out a breadbasket from Mother's cupboard. She was saying, "Mommy, can we use this basket? We're playing church!"

Children learn to mimic at an early age. In those years they are open to our values.

Bonnie had come home from a church service where the pastor had been raising pledges for a revival meeting. When her mother couldn't find her after dinner, she went looking. At last she found Bonnie in the chicken house with several hens cornered. She was saying to them, "Every one of you hens that'll promise to lay an egg today hold up your hand!"

Adult attitudes toward stewardship shape the attitude of children toward spiritual values. Are our habits worth mimicking?

Offertory Prayer
DEAR HEAVENLY FATHER:

Your plan shows wisdom much higher than ours, because:

> What I kept I lost.
> What I spent I had.
> What I gave I have!
> In Jesus' name, Amen.

245

Development and Use of Ritual in Pastoral Care

RITUAL AND PASTORAL CARE

Words have power. Some words have life-giving power. And when life-giving words are embraced in moments of profound meaning, the effect is eternal.

In the Wesleyan theological tradition there has always been an appreciation for the use of ritual. John Wesley, himself an Anglican cleric, made daily use of the *Book of Common Prayer.* When possible he participated daily in the Eucharist, encouraging the practice among the early Methodists in England.

Though Wesley himself designed and commended to the American church his "Sunday Services," based in large measure on the order of worship in the Anglican *Book of Common Prayer,* in practice the American Methodists made little use of the more elaborate rituals so loved by Wesley. It must be said that he invested in those rituals a deep spiritual reality and found them, not a distraction or a bother, but a means of grace and a source of deep and abiding meaning.

In the more primitive American settings of brush arbors and simple chapels, house-church gatherings, and itinerant circuit-riding preachers, such use of ritual seemed out of place and difficult to practice. Though many of the churches in the larger cities relied more on the "Sunday Services," the majority of the churches were less structured and more reliant on extempore formats and orders of service.

In even the most extempore Methodist settings, however, there was a deep appreciation of the need to participate at least occasionally in the sacraments of baptism and the Lord's Supper. Though not always done with great majesty, the sacraments were cherished, and in the minds of the people, the proper officiant contributed an important element to the significance of the rituals.

At the time of the Holiness awakenings that occurred near the end of the 19th century and the beginning of the 20th century, independent Holiness associations sprang up in many places across the United States and Canada, as well as in other nations. The fellowship and fervor within the various associations was intense. Worship, evangelism, and passionate emphasis on the deeper life were characteristic of the associations. One of the needs that seemed somewhat problematic, however, was the desire by many of those in the Holiness associations to participate in the sacraments of baptism and the Lord's Supper. A common concern was that without appropriate ecclesiastical training and endorsement, it was difficult to know who should be empowered to administer the sacraments to the people and what forms those celebrations should take.

The desire for proper endorsement and preparation of ministers who were legitimately able to serve and administer the sacraments led many to propose that their associations ought to consider forming a larger denominational body. Such a body, they felt, could give appropriate legitimacy to the preparation and oversight of ministers, thereby providing for more adequate pastoral care and the administration of the sacraments.

In time, such endorsement was established in many Wesleyan bodies. While the observance of the sacraments was desired, however, the resistance to ritualism continued. Churches that desired at least minimal form for the administration of the sacraments resisted allowing their worship services to routinely be encumbered with too much ritual.

While such resistance is understood as a justifiable reaction to an overuse of ritual in some traditions, the resistance also produced a distrust of ritual at some levels that stifled the consideration of its legitimate use as a means of spiritual formation, doctrinal clarity, and pastoral care.

There has been a recent return to more frequent uses of ritual by many congregations in the Wesleyan tradition, often especially among those populated by young adults seeking expressions of worship found in ancient forms. This has brought a new appreciation of the place of well-designed ritual in worship and in pastoral care.

At heart, the practice of pastoral care must be theologically driven. It is necessary for every pastor to found his or her practice on a carefully studied theological understanding of the work of ministry. The work of pastoral ministry is to point people to Christ, the Son of the Living God, who by His suffering on our behalf, provides us access to God by grace through faith. The presence of the Holy Spirit in the life of the Church is the essential resource for ministry. It is to this reality that the people of the Church are directed through the work of pastoral ministry.

One responsibility of the pastor is to work with families or individuals who are experiencing major life passages or spiritual breakthroughs. Those moments are open doors for ministry in ways that help people give voice to their experiences. Such occasions offer a level of pastoral care that is hardly available in any other circumstance. One of the tasks of pastoral care is to provide opportunities for, and experiences of, reflection on life passages that will enable appropriate avenues for new meanings to occur.

It is not the pastor's role to suggest how people ought to feel in those moments. Rather, it is to show how a particular situation or experience provides possibilities for spiritual growth and the appropriation of grace. Thus sensitive pastoral care should seek to give voice to the disorienting experiences in the lives of people in ways that enable them to constructively assimilate these experiences into their life journeys. Failure to offer this kind of assistance can leave people to deal with crises with inadequate coping mechanisms or poor theology and may lead to destructive beliefs or actions. Even a positive life passage, dealt with inappropriately, can become a limitation to a person's spiritual formation.

The purpose for this essay and the following section in this handbook is to recommend to pastors a means of developing and using ritual for use in pastoral care. The Church uses many rituals in the course of its corporate life together. The sacraments of baptism and the Lord's Supper are treasured rituals, often moments of profound spiritual encounter for the people of faith. But there are other rituals we cherish as well: marriage, the baptism or dedication of infants, the reception of church members, the dedication of buildings, and so on.

There is also a place for working with individuals, families, groups, or all the people of the congregation in developing new and/or unique and creative rituals that can give voice to moments of profound significance for which there are no other adequate means of expression.

A risk in pastoral care to those in crisis or experiencing major life change is that our efforts may be primarily functional, trying to "help." The greater need is to be *present*—to minister the consolations of Christ, the resources of the Word, to be a friend, a support. If the objective of pastoral care is the spiritual formation of the people to whom we minster, the manner in which we relate to them and to their needs will influence their openness to the possibility that God may do a deep, creative, sanctifying work in them. What is primary is not what we do, nor even what they do, but what God desires to do in them, for them, and through them. It is in light of what He accomplishes that expression may be found, that voice may be given, that words may come to have new meaning, and that a given life passage may be an occasion for profound spiritual growth.

Ritual, in order to have meaning and significance, must be related to an awakening of faith in the people who participate. There is a need in pastoral care to create and discover ways to aid in that awakening. The reality of God's gracious initiatives must be acknowledged. Ritual finds a way to embrace that reality, not create it.

The section that follows contains examples of created ritual in the context of pastoral care. The examples portray real-life people in real churches. The names are pseudonyms, and the circumstances a composite of several similar experiences. But the outcome in the development of each ritual is genuine, though illustrative. These rituals are not intended to be merely reproduced and used as they are. The value of the rituals was as much in the mutual effort used to create them as it was in the exercise of them.

May God, who through the Eternal Word spoke worlds into existence, enable you to use words to create worlds of meaning for the people to whom you minister the Word.

Jesse C. Middendorf
Overland Park, Kansas
September 2008

Ritual Developed for the Dedication of a Child

This ritual was developed in anticipation of the birth of a child born to a couple who had hoped for children for nearly a decade. Several pregnancies had ended in miscarriages, and medical and surgical remedies for the wife and mother were repeatedly attempted. After the most recent miscarriage only months prior to our meeting, the couple came to me with a cautious optimism that the current pregnancy was proceeding normally. The doctor had indicated that the complications that had occurred early in previous pregnancies did not seem to be happening in this one. After the first trimester, the pregnancy was evaluated as normal in every measure. All blood tests and amniotic fluid tests were normal, and the child was developing as expected. The couple was elated.

Soon, however, they were back in my office, struggling with the latest word from the doctor, who had told them on the previous day that a routine sonogram had revealed the presence of a cyst, perhaps more than one, in one lung of the developing child. The couple was frightened, devastated by the news, and struggling to know how to respond to this new development.

They were both devout and fervent believers, and as we talked, they began to recall passages of Scripture that had meant so much to them during previous struggles. Though frightened and concerned for the health of their child, they began to express their confidence that God was with them. They recalled their reliance on the story of Hannah's prayer after the birth of Samuel (1 Sam. 1:1-28). Soon they turned the conversation to the desire to plan the dedication service for their child.

The couple wanted the dedication to be a testimony to God's faithfulness throughout their long ordeal. They also wanted to use the event as a testimony to their family and friends that their child was a gift from God for which they accepted responsibility as stewards of His gracious gift.

As we discussed the ritual of dedication, I asked them if they would be interested in our developing a unique ritual of dedication for this child, given the long years of struggle and disappointment, and especially given the most recent developments. They readily agreed, and we made plans to remain in communication during the weeks remaining prior to the birth.

The following ritual is the result of the work done during those weeks. The child was born with the cysts still present, though otherwise healthy. The cysts did not prove to be life threatening, and within a few weeks of his birth, the little boy underwent successful surgery for the removal of the cysts, all proving to be nonmalignant. He is now a growing, happy, and very healthy boy. The service of dedication, held on a Sunday morning, was an experience of grace for everyone present.

A Developed Ritual for the Dedication of a Child

The parents and child will be presented to the pastor and the congregation by the children's pastor. He will usher them to the altar and then take his place beside the pastor. The pastor will then invite members of the families of the father and the mother to join the couple and their baby boy. A husband and wife, friends of the family for years, were asked to join the family at the altar as godparents. This godly older man and woman have taken a special interest in the couple during their years of struggle and disappointment, agreeing to serve as mentors and spiritual guides to the family.

Children's Pastor (Reads Matt. 19:13-15.)

Pastor: Dear friends, the dedication of a child is always a sacred occasion for the church. In this ritual we express the covenantal reality that this child is a gift of God and is at this moment covered by prevenient grace in light of the atoning work of Christ on our behalf.

_____ and _____ *[names of the father and mother],* the presentation of your child for dedication is much more than mere formality and ritual for you. This is the culmination of years of prayer and anticipation. Your son is an acknowledged gift of God to you, and you take your stewardship of this gift seriously. We have discussed this moment on several occasions, and you have desired that today be an opportunity for you to publically affirm your gratitude to God for entrusting this child to your care.

In presenting your child for dedication, you have expressed your desire that he be nurtured in the faith, that he be taught to be responsive to the grace of God, that he come to have a dynamic and personal relationship with Jesus Christ, and that his life be lived in obedient service to Christ.

In order that this outcome may be possible, it will be your duty as parents to carefully direct his mind to the Scriptures, to mold his life by example and admonition, and to teach him to value the disciplines of holy living, godly attitudes, and wholesome relationships.

You must teach him also to delight in the love and tenderness of God. He will need to be nurtured toward a level of trust and confidence that will come only as you demonstrate those characteristics yourselves.

In your journey through the heartaches and frustrations of the past several years you have come to treasure a passage of Scripture that has become your testimony and is your expression of the dedication of your son to God. Will you now share it with your family and friends who are gathered here today?

Parents (in unison): From the words of Hannah, the mother of Samuel, the prophet of God, we affirm our confidence in the provision of God, and in the words of her prayer we affirm: "I prayed for this child, and the LORD has granted me what I asked of him. So now I give him to the LORD. For his whole life he will be given over to the LORD" (1 Sam. 1:27-28, NIV).

> At this point in the ceremony, the mother read a very personal and tender letter she had written to her as yet unborn child following the discovery of the complications related to his lungs. It was a testimony of her own journey from frustration and fear over the inability to have a child, through the joy of a normal and healthy pregnancy, to the despair at the news of the complications, and finally to the rest and hope of faith

that God was able to provide needed grace for every eventuality.

Pastor (to the families of the parents): You have heard the testimony and commitment of _____ and _____ *[names of father and mother]*. I now ask you to affirm your prayerful support for them and for their son, _____ *[name of child]*. Will each of you seek to support and encourage these parents in their duties and responsibilities, and will you nurture _____ *[name of child]* by godly example and prayer? If so, please answer, "I will."

Family (in unison): I will.

Pastor (to the congregation): You have heard the words of testimony and commitment made by _____ and _____ *[names of father and mother]*. You have heard the words of support expressed by the families who surround them. I now ask you, the congregation: Will you, as the family of God, seek to nurture this family in its growth and development? Will you covenant to pray for them and to so live before them and with them that the grace of God will enfold them through you and that the power of the Holy Spirit will enable _____ and _____ *[names of father and mother]* to fulfill their duties as parents to their son, _____ *[name of child]*? If you will do so, please answer, "We will."

Congregation *(in unison):* We will.

The parents will now present the child to the pastor for the dedicatory prayer. At the request of the parents, the prayer of dedication will be followed by anointing the child with oil and a prayer for healing. At this time the pastor will call for the elders present in the service to join him at the altar for the dedicatory prayer and for the prayer for healing. The children's pastor will assist the pastor, holding the oil for anointing the child. The pastor will take the child in his arms, address the child, and then pray.

Pastor: _____ *[name of child],* you are a gift from God to your parents. They are now bringing you back to Him as a gift of love from them. And now, with your parents, and in the presence of the congregation, we dedicate you to God, in the name of the Father and of the Son and of the Holy Spirit.

Gracious Father, this sacred moment is filled with the glory of Your presence. As godly Simeon praised You when he held the infant Jesus, so I lift my voice in praise for Your gracious gift of this child to _____ and _____ *[names of father and mother].* You have entrusted them with a priceless gift, and they have acknowledged Your trust. They have sought Your guidance, and they have committed themselves to You as stewards of this precious gift.

I pray for Your wisdom, Your protection, Your guidance, and Your delight in this child. May he early come to discover what it means to know You as Father, and may the graces that have filled the lives of his parents be bestowed on his tender heart. Grant that he may be the occasion of thousands to come to know You, by his life, his teaching, and his obedient service.

Father, what this child becomes rests in great measure in the hands and hearts of these parents. May they be wholly committed to knowing and doing Your will in their lives so that this son of theirs will always have a godly example to follow. May their home be open to the needy of the world so that their son may learn the joy of serving others. And may their hearts be tender to the lost of the world so that he may know the joy of leading others to know You.

This we pray in confidence in Your love for these three.

And now, Father, we continue in Your presence as we anoint this child for healing.

As the children's pastor anoints the child with oil, the elders join in by laying their hands on the child, on the parents, or on the shoulders of a minister standing near them.

Children's Pastor: _____ *[name of child]*, I lay my hands upon you and anoint you with oil in the name of the Father and of the Son and of the Holy Spirit, asking our Lord Jesus Christ to sustain you with His presence, to drive away all sickness of body and spirit, and to give you life and peace in such measure that you will serve Him in this life, and in the life to come may have eternal life. Amen.

Pastor: And now, Heavenly Father, we come to You in confidence, in humility, and in faith in Your Word. Heal this child of all disease. Deliver him from all harm. Preserve him in health and well-being. As he grows in wisdom, in stature, and in favor with God and man, use his gifts and graces for the advancement of Your kingdom. Honor the trust and commitment of these parents with grace for the days ahead, and may they sense a renewal of strength and hope through Your holy presence. This we ask in the name of the resurrected and reigning Christ. Amen.

Ritual for the Reaffirmation of a Marriage Covenant and the Renewal of a Family

Occasionally a pastor will have the privilege of working with a marriage in the process of being rebuilt. Often in such situations healing is needed not only between husband and wife but also between them and other members of the family and/or close friends.

This ritual was developed with a couple who desired to invite their teen and young adult children and their parents to a private gathering in the sanctuary of the church where they could reaffirm their commitments to one another after a period of disarray, stress, and separation. Both husband and wife were professional people whose pursuits of success and recognition had robbed them of time together, had weakened their spiritual commitments, and had alienated them from family members, who felt neglected, even abandoned.

To their credit, they had insisted that the family keep its ties to the church, but their own involvement became sporadic, punctuated by long periods of time away on trips for business and pleasure. They continued to support the church financially and spoke of the church affirmatively and encouragingly whenever anyone from the church was with them.

While they were, to the casual observer, doing well, though overcommitted, their homelife was in shambles. They each later acknowledged that this was more obvious to others in the family than to themselves. Caught up in the whirlwind of busy schedules and increasingly independent young adult and teenage children, they were stunned when, finally, their teenage children refused to attend church any longer and began participating in destructive and dangerous behaviors and relationships.

The tensions boiled over into deeply felt and openly expressed recriminations toward one another. They struggled briefly for equilibrium but over time tired of the ongoing and increasing tension. After several months of growing bitterness toward one another, the couple seemed paralyzed and unable to make a decision about what to do next. He finally announced that he was going to move into an apartment, and they began to discuss the possibility of divorce.

Though both had grown up in devout homes, they had neglected the priorities and values with which they were raised. It was not until one of them decided to move out of the home that they realized what was happening. Within hours of one another, unknown to the other, each had called me and asked for time to meet with me. Both were in tears when they arrived and deeply remorseful over the state of affairs in their home.

Our meetings were immediately productive. Each acknowledged his or her own part in what had occurred, and each confessed to the other the regret felt over the situation, openly acknowledging his or her need for God's gracious forgiveness. Each assured the other that no inappropriate relationships had occurred outside of the marriage.

The family was immediately very consistent in their attendance at church, the teen children returning as well, albeit somewhat reluctantly. Even in their reluctance, the children were obviously relieved to see the family dynamics improving.

After a few weeks of consistent improvement, the couple began to discuss with me how they might make a very intentional expression of the reaffirmation of their spiritual commitments and of their marriage. They wanted to use this as a time to bring healing to other relationships as well. We talked about a number of options and finally settled on the development of a ceremony that would enable the family to take part in a service of covenant renewal. The "Wesley Covenant Service" (see pages 211-25) and traditional marriage vows provided a model for our discussion.

One salient feature of this service was the responsibility felt by the pastor to embrace the privilege and the authority to pronounce forgiveness for two people who had genuinely sought to express their deep and profound repentance toward God for their failure. As we worked together in the development of this ritual, they took a very vulnerable step by speaking so openly of their failure, calling it sin, and humbly acknowledging their need for grace. In the very development of the ritual they found a genuine measure of peace and restoration.

Working with the children of the family was also necessary to determine how comfortable they were about participating in the service. They had already experienced the profound changes that were occurring in their parents, so their willingness to participate grew into a genuine anticipation.

Because of the nature of the ritual, implementing it in a public worship service did not seem prudent. However, it would have been possible to encourage the couple to invite members of the church who were friends and mentors to be present as representatives of the community of faith.

This ritual was designed to give voice to people who genuinely wanted to say some very important things about their own spiritual journey to their family but did not know how to do so. It became a turning point for the family.

Ritual of Covenant Renewal

The couple invited their family to gather in the sanctuary. Because of the impact of their crisis on three generations, both their children and their parents were invited to participate in the ritual.

As the ceremony began, the couple and the pastor were standing at the altar, and all others were seated. Each person present received a copy of the order of service, and a brief explanation of the service was given. All present were invited to participate in the ritual as indicated in the program. Each had had opportunity to participate in developing the segment in which he or she was invited to respond. Each was encouraged to participate in the service only to the extent that he or she was comfortable in allowing the service to voice the things felt in his or her own heart.

Pastor: _____ and _____ *[names of husband and wife],* you have invited your family to join you in this service of renewal of your covenant of marriage. This is a sacred occasion for you, one about which we have prayed and planned for weeks.

You do not take this occasion lightly. It is for you an evening of both joy and pain.

There is the pain of your struggle, a long journey away from things you once cherished. There were others who were wounded in your journey, and in the months since you each began to hunger after God at a new level in your lives, you have brought them into your hearts, shared your concern for them, and have sought their forgiveness and their help in the recovery of things damaged or misplaced.

But there is also the joy of your discovery of the depths of grace extended to you by God, the grace each of you has received from the other, and the grace extended to you by family and friends.

This will not be an easy evening, nor is it intended to merely allow you to assuage your own consciences while you force the reemergence of forgotten pain on others. But you will find this a healing experience because you are establishing a new level of responsibility and accountability between the two of you, between each of you and the Lord Jesus Christ, and between you and the members of your family.

I invite each of us to join _____ and _____ *[names of husband and wife]* as we open our hearts to God in the prayer for purity (printed):

"Almighty God, to you all hearts are open, all desires known, and from you no secrets are hid: Cleanse the thoughts of our hearts by the inspiration of your Holy Spirit, that we may perfectly love you, and worthily magnify your holy Name; through Christ our Lord. Amen."[26]

Pastor: _____ and _____ *[names of husband and wife]:* [Thirty] years ago the two of you stood before a congregation, and in the presence of God, exchanged your vows and entered into the covenant of

Christian marriage. God blessed your relationship, and you took great delight in one another. Each encouraged the other's growth and celebrated the successes each of you enjoyed. You accomplished a great deal and were admired by all your family and friends. Over time you experienced the joy of bringing children into the world, watching them grow, encouraging them, and challenging them. You provided for their education and insisted on their involvement in the church.

Though you were busy, you remained loyal to one another, and neither ever feared, even during your worst moments, that the other had been unfaithful to your marriage vows. For that we are all grateful.

But we are here tonight because you have invited us here. You have asked me as your pastor to assist you as you acknowledge before God and your family a very difficult part of your journey. You have come to seek and to acknowledge His forgiveness and to seek and to acknowledge the forgiveness of your family.

But you also come to enter into a covenant of faithfulness to God that you are asking me and your family to witness and to participate in, in order that you may hold yourselves accountable to Him, to one another, and to your family.

We have talked in depth about this evening, and we have each participated in structuring the things we will say. We will begin with the reading of scripture.

SCRIPTURE READING BY A SELECTED MEMBER OF THE
FAMILY

1 John 1:5—2:6

Pastor: _____ and _____ *[names of
husband and wife],* you have come before God in brokenness and repentance. Your hearts have been broken
by the realization of your failure and your blindness.
You have acknowledged to one another those things
that bring you grief, and you have sought the mercy of
God. How do you desire to acknowledge your sense of
need for God's grace?

Couple (in unison): We acknowledge a deep sense
that we have failed. We have betrayed God, betrayed
one another, and betrayed our family. We desire to call
it what it was to God and what it became to us: We have
sinned. We see ourselves as sinners in need of a Savior.
The Spirit of God has awakened us. We sense our un-
doneness and stand in humble, honest sorrow for our
willfulness and sin.

We also acknowledge that our brokenness alone will
not save us, nor will our determination to do better.

We need the gracious gift of God's mercy, His forgiveness, and His Spirit's enabling.

We repent of our sin and turn from it wholeheart-
edly.

We throw ourselves on His mercy.

We trust only in the suffering and resurrection of

Jesus Christ on our behalf as sufficient basis for our redemption.

Pastor: Having confessed your need of Christ, take Christ.

Take Him by faith.

Take His grace that has called you to himself.

Take His mercy that is extended to you.

Take His peace and His joy!

He has forgiven you!

Couple: Thanks be to God!

All (in unison):

Dear friends, if our hearts do not condemn us, we have confidence before God and receive from him anything we ask, because we obey his commands and do what pleases him. And this is his command: to believe in the name of his Son, Jesus Christ, and to love one another as he commanded us. Those who obey his commands live in them, and he in them. And this is how we know that he lives in us: We know it by the Spirit he gave us. (1 John 3:21-24, NIV)

Pastor: I invite you now to renew your covenant of marriage.

_____ *[name of husband]:* will you renew your covenant of marriage to _____ *[name of wife]?*

Will you love her, cherish her, honor and keep her, in sickness or in health, in plenty or in want?

Will you be faithful to her, and forsaking all other human loyalties, keep yourself only for her, so long as you both will live?

Husband: I will.

Pastor: _____ [name of wife], will you renew your covenant of marriage to _____ [name of husband]?

Will you love him, cherish him, honor and keep him, in sickness or in health, in plenty or in want?

Will you be faithful to him, and forsaking all other human loyalties, keep yourself only for him, so long as you both will live?

Wife: I will.

Pastor: And now, what do you wish to say to your family?

Husband: To you, our children, I wish to say openly what I have said to each of you in private.

I seek your forgiveness for my self-centeredness and for my preoccupation with those things that robbed you of my attention and my nurture.

I have failed to provide the support and affirmation that you deserved.

I have failed to model the Christian character you needed to see in me.

I have loved you, but you have not known it.

I cherish and love you deeply, and covenant with you that to the best of my ability, I will be the father you deserve and expect and will lead by example and admonition but not by demand.

I want you to see Christ in me and will do my best to follow Him so that to whatever extent you desire to do so, you may follow me.

Wife: I seek your forgiveness for the days when you felt alone and I felt that duty called me elsewhere.

I seek your forgiveness for the times when you wanted to talk and I demanded that you "get busy."

I seek your forgiveness for the times when your schedule and my schedule made me think it was your schedule that should change.

I told you I loved you but lived at a distance from you.

You sometimes told me you needed me. I did not realize how desperately I needed you.

I thought it was enough to talk to Jesus about you. I now know that I should have taken the time to talk to you about Jesus.

I ask your forgiveness, and I promise you my love, my time, and my schedule.

The Children: Mother and Dad, we acknowledge the work of God in your lives. We have seen Him at work in your relationship and in our home. We accept your repentance, and we offer you our forgiveness. We will walk with you, grow with you, and love you.

Give us time with you, and give us time to grow. Show God to us, but let us seek Him for ourselves.

Husband and Wife: Mothers and fathers, you have taught us better than we have lived. You have loved God and shown Him to us. You have prayed for us and admonished us.

We have not always heeded your words, but we have not been away from the effect of your prayers. God in His mercy has restored us to himself. We ask for your forgiveness and pledge you our faithfulness to pass the godly heritage we received along to our children.

Parents: Thanks be to God for His work in your lives.

May His peace fill your hearts and His love fill your home.

May you find ways to honor Him through selfless service.

May you find grace to follow Him through obedient response to His leadership.

May your children find Him first in your lives and your lives find Him first in your hearts.

May your love for Jesus be the pattern of your love for all others.

We bless you and we honor you, in the name of God.

Pastor: And now, as the apostle Paul wrote in his letter to the church at Thessalonica:

> May the God of peace himself sanctify you entirely; and may your spirit and soul and body be kept sound and blameless at the coming of our Lord Jesus Christ. The one who calls you is faithful, and he will do this. Beloved, pray for us. (1 Thess. 5:23-25, NRSV)

The family was invited to stand together and sing "The Doxology."

Ritual for the Celebration
of a Family Heritage

This ritual was developed to assist a family through a very difficult life passage. An aged mother, nearing 100 years of age, was bedfast, unable to care for her needs without assistance, and in obviously declining health. She was alert but was severely limited in her ability to move or stand due to the crippling effects of arthritis. She had lived on her own until recent months and was now under the care of her daughter and son-in-law. Realizing the dangers of her living alone, these two had relinquished the comfort of their own bedroom and had moved the mother into their home.

The family knew that the health of their beloved mother and grandmother was failing. They desired to find some way to celebrate her life and her faith with her before her passing, and she expressed her own desire to say some very important things to her daughter and her family, to her granddaughters and their husbands, and to her great-granddaughters.

After a discussion with the daughter and then with her mother, we began to plan a time when we could give meaningful structure to such a celebration. I worked with several of the family members over time, and the following Family Ritual for Celebration and Blessing was designed. While it may seem a bit formal and stilted, the order was not intended to be followed rigidly but to be followed in a relaxed and informal atmosphere in the home. The structure, which could be more or less adhered to, provided meaningful guidance for what the members of the family intended the evening to accomplish.

The depths of pastoral care required for a ritual of this nature are obvious. It could only be developed in a setting where a deep level of trust and confidence existed between the pastor and the members of the family. Some of the issues that had to be discussed required candor and unshakable trust in the character and the faith of the people involved. Even the development of the ritual was a remarkable experience of bonding for all participants. A printed order with appropriate prompts and written scripture passages was prepared for use in this gathering.

A Family Ritual for Celebration and Blessing
SCRIPTURE READING: *Gen. 48:8-11*

Pastor: You are an extraordinarily blessed family. You have a godly heritage that extends back for generations and holds the promise of fulfilling the Old Testament assurance of the blessing of God on the family of the faithful to a thousand generations (Exod. 34:6-7).

_____ *[name of the mother],* you received a godly heritage. You embraced it, adorned it with your life, and you and your late husband have faithfully and graciously passed it along.

_____ and _____ *[names of the daughter and son-in-law],* you have been stewards of this heritage for another generation. It has defined you. You have embraced its values and priorities and carefully taught them to your own family. You have faithfully passed it along.

_____ and _____ *[names of the*

granddaughter and her husband], you, too, have received a wonderful and godly heritage, and you and your family are cherishing it. You have had the courage to examine it, to test it, and to embrace it. Now you, too, are faithfully passing it along.

_____ and _____ *[names of the great-granddaughters]*, you have received a priceless and wonderful Christian heritage. It is a legacy that has been carefully tended by the generations before you. You have already begun to grasp it, and it is shaping you into the persons God wills you to become. It will be your opportunity and privilege to examine this heritage, to embrace it, to instill it with new life and vigor, and to pass it along to your children and families.

SCRIPTURE READING: *2 Tim. 2:1-2*

Pastor: Now, I ask each generation to express your gratitude to God for the gift of His grace to you in Christ Jesus by briefly telling everyone how and when you came to personal faith in Christ.

Each person, having been asked and assisted in advance to prepare a brief written account of his or her coming to personal faith in Christ, was prepared to read it aloud to the group.

UNISON SCRIPTURE READING (printed): *Ps. 103*

After the reading, the pastor was to pray a prayer of gratitude for the stories, for God's faithfulness to His Word, and for the fact that the relationship with God through Jesus Christ is available to each generation with a remarkable freshness and meaning.

Pastor: Now, I will ask each generation to express to the generation immediately preceding it one aspect of your heritage for which you are particularly grateful.

Each person was to read a brief previously prepared statement that described the personal impact one aspect of his or her heritage has had on his or her life.

Pastor: Now, I will ask _____ *[name of the mother]* to bless each generation by placing her hand on each couple and pronouncing a blessing.

This was to have been previously prepared, with the help of the daughter and the pastor, so that the statement could be personal, succinct, and clear.

Pastor: Now, I will ask all of you to gather around your mother and grandmother and bless her in the name of the Lord.

A reading had been prepared for them to read in unison.

Family: [Mother, Grandmother, or Great-grandmother], we bless you in the name of the Lord. Your love and your example have instructed and sustained us. Your faithfulness to your home, to your family, to your church, and to our world has been a model and an inspiration. Your life is a treasure we cherish in gratitude to God.

We commit you to His care and love, assuring you of our continued love and concern and our active involvement in your care. We promise you our prayers, our presence, our support, our attention, and our loyalty.

"Now [we] commit you to God and to the word of his grace, which can build you up and give you an inheritance among all those who are sanctified" (Acts 20:32, NIV).

HYMN: "Great Is Thy Faithfulness"

Ritual for the Dedication of a Home

This ritual was created in consultation with a young seminarian and his wife who, upon graduation from seminary, accepted an assignment as church planters. They had attended our church for several years, working in a variety of ministries and exercising a maturing and effective influence on other families in the church.

Our local church and the district cooperated in sponsoring the new church, and the pastor and wife requested that we work together to develop a dedication ritual for the home they were purchasing in their target community. The home was to be the site of the initial gatherings for the new church, and they wanted the dedication to be a time when they and the small core group could commit themselves to one another for this adventure in faith in this new setting.

The dedication ritual was planned over a number of meetings with them. During this time they had already begun to meet with the core group of families in the area to which they were moving. They continued to worship with the mother church for several weeks while they met with the core group on weeknights, preparing and equipping them for the anticipated start date for the new church.

The dedication ceremony and the ritual, while simple and straightforward, included the opportunity for several participants to express their anticipation for what lay ahead in the church planting endeavor. Guests included district leadership as well as friends, prayer supporters, and participants in the new church plant. Guests were invited from the community in which the home was located, including nearby pastors of other churches. Several of them came to welcome the new pastor and his wife.

The evening reflected a festive and happy atmosphere but was also filled with a sense of significance because of the apparent openness of the community to the church plant. This was initially not planned as a "church planting event." The couple had only desired a small gathering of friends for the dedication of their new home. However, as the excitement in the community began to build, the couple decided to incorporate into this event the opportunity to introduce their neighbors to the plans for the future. It began to take on a significance not anticipated in our early conversations. Creating this ritual became a missional imperative.

The ceremony that follows is substantially as it was designed and utilized on that special evening. Note the ways in which the words of the ritual provide the opportunity to paint a vision for the future. As guests arrived, each was given a copy of the folder in which the order of service was printed.

A Service of Dedication for the
Home of _____ and _____

[Names of Husband and Wife]

ORDER OF SERVICE

WELCOME   Host Couple
    Introductions
    Presentation of Our Vision

PRAYER OF THANKSGIVING   Husband

LITANY OF DEDICATION
Scripture: Mark 10:23-30

Minister: _____ and _____ *[names of husband and wife],* to what calling do you commit yourselves and your home?

Couple: With clarity in understanding the leadership of the Holy Spirit, we dedicate ourselves to the fulfillment of His calling on our lives as husband and wife. Having left all competing loyalties and relationships behind, we make it our aim to know Christ, to be His disciples in our personal lives, and to be His instruments in our community.

We commit ourselves to the fulfillment of His call to ministry in the name of Jesus Christ and through the Church _____ *[name of church].*

We commit ourselves to the ministry of church planting in the town of _____, with certainty in the leadership of the Spirit and in celebration of His faithfulness.

SCRIPTURE: Matt. 5:14-15

Minister: To what ends and for what purpose do you wish to dedicate this house?

All: As a fitting and pleasant place where this pastor and his family can make their home.

As a place where study and meditation on the Holy Scripture may be pursued.

As a place where Christian fellowship may be had,

where we may share both our joys and our sorrows, our successes and our shortcomings, and where we may strengthen the ties that bind our hearts in Christian love.

As a place where the confidential counsel of God's ministering servant can be found.

And as a quiet and comfortable place of refuge and relief to which God's servant can return when at times the duties and responsibilities of Christian ministry bear heavily.

To these ends, and to the glory of God, we now dedicate this home.

SCRIPTURE: Isa. 32:17-18

All Shall Pray in Unison: To live with You, O Lord, is to be at home with ourselves. Now be with us, we pray, as we dedicate this house as a home for _____ and _____ *[names of husband and wife].* Bless these personal things of taste and choice that put the mark of these particular people upon it and make it theirs. May it be a place of shelter and protection, of rest and healing, of warmth and hospitality. And may Your embracing love be seen and felt in all celebrations, daily chores, hard decisions, and shared glories that will occur here. As it will become the storehouse of blessed memories, make it also a place for growth in grace. We pray in the name of Him who has prepared a place for us, in whose house are many rooms, even Jesus Christ our Lord. Amen.

All: (Recite the Helen Taylor poem on pages 151-52)
CLOSING PRAYER

Notes

1. Walter Brueggemann, *Cadences of Home* (Louisville, Ky.: Westminster John Knox Press, 1997), 12, 21, 42.

2. John Telford, ed., *The Letters of John Wesley* (London: Epworth Press, 1931), letter to John Smith, 1746, 2:77-78.

3. Brueggemann, *Cadences of Home,* 79.

4. J. Kenneth Grider, *A Wesleyan-Holiness Theology* (Kansas City: Beacon Hill Press of Kansas City, 1994), 502-3.

5. *Manual, 1993-1997: Church of the Nazarene* (Kansas City: Nazarene Publishing House), 28.

6. Rob L. Staples, *Outward Sign and Inward Grace* (Kansas City: Beacon Hill Press of Kansas City, 1991), 179-80.

7. H. Ray Dunning, *Grace, Faith, and Holiness* (Kansas City: Beacon Hill Press of Kansas City, 1988), 550.

8. Staples, *Outward Sign and Inward Grace,* 180.

9. Ibid.

10. See *Book of Common Prayer* (New York: Church Hymnal Corporation, 1979), 323, 355, for alternate versions of this prayer, known as the Collect for Purity.

11. Ibid.

12. Ibid., 507.

13. Ibid., 323, 355, for alternate versions of prayer.

14. Adapted from *Dedication Services for Every Occasion* compiled by Manfred Holck Jr. (Valley Forge, Pa.: Judson Press, 1984), 39-40. Reprinted by permission of the publisher. 1-800-4-JUDSON. www.judsonpress.com.

15. Ibid., 91-92.

16. Adapted from "The Hanging of the Greens" by Sally Rhodes Ahner. Copyright © 1986 by Abingdon Press. Used by permission.

17. Excerpts from *The Book of Blessings,* additional blessings for use in the United States of America © 1988 United States Conference of Catholic Bishops, Washington, D.C. Adapted and used with permission from the copyright owner. All rights reserved.

18. Ibid.

19. Adapted from *From Hope to Joy* by Don Saliers © 1984 by Abingdon Press. Used by permission.

20. James R. Spruce, ed., *A Pastor's Worship Resource—for Advent, Lent, and Other Occasions* (Kansas City: Beacon Hill Press of Kansas City, 1987), 67-74.

21. Ibid., 123-33.

22. Prayer by Michael J. O'Donnell, *The United Methodist Book of Worship.* Copyright © 1992 by The United Methodist Publishing House. Used by permission.

23. Ken Bible, comp., *Wesley Hymns* (Kansas City: Lillenas Publishing Co., 1982), A-2-10.

24. Spruce, *Pastor's Worship Resource,* 175-82.

25. Ibid., 183-90.

26. *Book of Common Prayer,* 355.

Rituals/Ceremonies in
Manual/2005-9 Church of the Nazarene

For ministers and worship leaders who use the *Manual of the Church of the Nazarene,* the following rituals in this book may be found as numbered in that source:

800.1   The Baptism of Believers

800.2   The Baptism of Infants or Young Children (Rite Two)

800.3   The Dedication of Infants or Young Children

800.4   The Dedication of Infants or Young Children (Ritual for Single Parent or Guardian)

801   The Reception of Church Members

802   The Sacrament of the Lord's Supper (Rite One)

803   Matrimony (Rite One)

804   The Funeral Service

805   Installation of Officers

806   Church Dedications (Rite Two)

Printed in the USA
CPSIA information can be obtained
at www.ICGtesting.com
LVHW011112151124
796726LV00020B/250

9 780834 124578